LUIGI PIRANDELLO

General Editor: Robert Rietty

LUIGI PIRANDELLO

Collected Plays

Volume Three

THE RULES OF THE GAME
EACH IN HIS OWN WAY
GRAFTED
THE OTHER SON

CALDER PUBLICATIONS · RIVERRUN PRESS
Paris · London · New York

This edition first published in 1992 in Great Britain by
Calder Publications Limited
9-15 Neal Street, London WC2H 9TU

And in the United States of America in 1992 by
Riverrun Press Inc
1170 Broadway, New York NY 10001

British Library Cataloguing in Publication Data
Pirandello, Luigi 1867–1936
  Vol. 3
  Collected plays.
  1. Italian drama
  I. Title   II. Rietty, Robert
  852′.912

  ISBN 0-7145-4181-8

Library of Congress Cataloging in Publication Data
Pirandello, Luigi, 1867–1936.
  Collected plays.

  Translation from the Italian.
  Bibliography: v. 3, p. 218
  Contents: —v. 3 The rules of the game.
  Each in his own way. Grafted. The other son.
  1. Pirandello, Luigi, 1867–1936—Translations into English. I. Rietty, Robert. II. Title.
PQ4835.I7A2 1992   852′.912   86-27977
ISBN 0-7145-4181-8 (v. 3)

Typeset in 10/11 pt Times by Pure Tech Corporation, Pondicherry, India.
Printed in Great Britain by Whitstable Litho Printers Ltd., Whitstable, Kent.

CONTENTS

INTRODUCTION

Surprisingly little seems to be known in England about Luigi
Pirandello who died in 1936, and of whom *The Times* said: 'It
is largely to him that the theatre owes its liberation, for good or
ill, from what Desmond MacCarthy called "the inevitable limi-
tations of the modern drama, the falsifications which result from
cramming scenes into acts and tying incidents down to times
and places." ' Only a few of his major works have been published in English to date and as a result there is a tendency to
classify Pirandello as a purely intellectual writer, prone to 'cerebral gymnastics' and most difficult for an actor to interpret.
Those who find him so might first study a little the life of the
man and in so doing they may reach a better understanding of
Pirandello the dramatist.

Pirandello was born at Caos in Sicily in 1867. He studied
letters at Palermo University and later in Rome. For many years
he taught at a girls' school, living in comparative poverty and
growing steadily unhappier in his work. His marriage ended in
disaster when his wife became mentally unbalanced and had to
be sent to a mental institution. His literary efforts began with
poems, short stories and later he wrote novels; he did not start
writing seriously for the theatre until 1915 at the age of forty-
eight, after which he gave to the stage no fewer than forty-three
plays in Italian and several in Sicilian.

For a number of years he was in charge of his own theatrical
company, which had as its leaders Ruggero Ruggeri and Marta
Abba, and many of his plays were written as tailor-made ar-
ticles for them and for the rest of his group. Despite the severe
lack of finance, he never succumbed to writing plays which

conformed to the style and idiom of the more successful dramatists of his time. He deliberately created anti-heroes. His protagonists are like 'soldiers who have been beaten in their first battle and have no belief in the future!'

Having lost a considerable sum of money with his own company, and become greatly disillusioned because his native Italy considered him 'too original for the box office', (often his plays were translated and performed abroad long before they saw the footlights in their own language) and already almost seventy, Pirandello suddenly announced that Europe had grown too old for him, that it could boast of only one other young brain (Bernard Shaw), and that he would take himself off to a country of new ideas—and then journeyed to America.

Pirandello was a fiery, passionate man who had reached his own particular outlook on life through adversity and years of tortured wondering at the true significance of reality. His primary concern was with the illusions and self-deceptions of mankind and the nature of identity. His works grew—as Eric Bentley points out—'from his own torment, and through his genius they came to speak for all the tormented and potentially to all the tormented, that is, to all men.' He delighted in creating an unusual but logistical situation—developing it seemingly illogically—and by continually tossing the coin until both sides had been clearly revealed, managing to convince his audience that his unconventional and not very credible treatment was in fact wholly logical and convincing.

Many of his plays were written in the style known to the Italians as 'grottesco': comedies developed tragically or tragedies developed comically. Nearly all spring from intensely dramatic situations—situations in which passion, love and tragedy make their presence strongly felt.

In England theatre productions of his works have been few and far between, and this may be due partly to the fact that producers and actors, when faced with a play of his, sometimes assume: 'he is going to be far too difficult for the audience so it will be up to us to put that right!' By approaching the text with the preconceived notion that a particular interpretation must shine like a beacon between author and audience in order

to elucidate matters, one often succeeds merely in confusing the
issue further. There have been examples of this author's brilliantly cynical humour, behind whose mask we are meant to see
our own selves, being deliberately distorted to the level of
unacceptable farce in an attempt to 'clarify'.

If Pirandello's plays were approached more simply, were permitted to play *themselves* more, and did not have the Latin
sentiment and human compassion ironed out by their interpre-
ters, perhaps the fear that one may not be able to follow him
would be removed from the minds of many of our theatregoers.
It would be found that his comedies, as Kenneth Tynan wrote:
'wear their fifty-odd years as if they were swaddling clothes',
and his works might then find themselves a niche in our com-
mercial theatre.

In presenting the complete dramatic works of Luigi Pirandello, we have attempted to hold to the line of simplicity in translation, avoiding the temptation of so many adaptors to reconstruct
the author's statements in the light in which they themselves
see them. Many translations offered to us have been by people
with little or no knowledge of Italian, who have relied on a
commissioned literal translation which they have rephrased in
their own style. This is a method which should be severely
frowned upon.

Pirandello's plays often leave the audience with an uneasy
feeling that the situation is not concluded and that we have not
wholly understood all we have seen. We feel the need to discuss
the play and search for the real truth among the various aspects
of it which have been depicted for us.

In many of his plays, events do not take place before our eyes:
they have already occurred before the rise of the curtain. It is
as though we are aware of an immutable past awaiting judgment
. . . it weighs on the minds of the characters in the drama and
they cannot abandon or dismiss it. They are caught up in a
'prison of fact'. As Leône Gala says in *The Rules of the Game*:
'When a fact has happened, it stands there, like a prison, shutting you in.'

Pirandello seems determined never to allow his audience to
be satisfied. For him, the spectators are no inert mass which

revives and becomes articulate only after the curtain has fallen. No—they have to be awakened, shaken up and agitated while in their seats and made to become involved with the actors. The auditorium is to be part of the stage and the listener to take part in the discussion; to be filled with doubt and uncertainty.

Pirandello constantly reverses the coin, revolves the situation. He never intervenes to clarify: 'the enigma must remain an enigma, and at the end there is to be no conclusion, rather a question mark.' As Giovanni Macchia, an eminent authority on the maestro, says: 'it is impossible to love Pirandello, but then the destiny of all artistes today is not to make themselves loved, but to be oppressed and tortured. And among the tortured, the spectator is not to be spared.' As to his protagonists, they are not tragic heroes, but miserable sad objects worthy only of pity, derision or commiseration.

The Rules of the Game ('Il giuoco delle parti') first appeared in 1918. Time and again Pirandello shows us that 'in every human being there lurks a mass of contradictory personalities which—like a volcano—must finally erupt when one of those personalities attempts to force its way into the outer air.'

In 'Il giuoco delle parti' Leone gives an illuminating description of this multiple personality. Speaking to Guido about his wife Silia, he says: 'You're probably unaware of all the riches there are in her . . . qualities of mind and spirit you would never believe to be hers—because you know only one facet of her character, from which you have built up your idea of what is for you, and always will be, the real and only Silia. You wouldn't think it possible, for example, for Silia to go about her housework some mornings carefree, relaxed, happily singing or humming to herself. But she does, you know. I used to hear her sometimes, going from room to room, singing in a sweet little quavering voice, like a child's. A different woman. I'm not saying that just for the sake of saying it. Really a different woman—without knowing it! For a few moments when she is out of herself, she is just a child, singing. And if you could see how she sits sometimes, absorbed, gazing into space: a distant, living glow reflected in her eyes, and unconsciously smoothing her hair with idly straying fingers. Who is she then? Not the

Silia you know—another Silia, a Silia that can't live because she is unknown to herself, since no one has ever said to her "I love you when you are like that; that's the way I want you always to be." '

Leone has philosophically accepted his role as the 'betrayed husband', but his serene indifference irritates the sensual and hysterical Silia and, when fate plays into her hands, she devises a cunning way to rid herself of her husband once and for all.

In a *colpa di scena* Leone turns the tables on her in a brilliantly logical manner and despite his adopted mask of indifference, bursts into violent anger against Silia ... stunning the audience by this sudden transformation, and producing a wholly unexpected climax.

'*Il giuoco delle parti*' is one of the most brilliant and characteristic of Pirandello's plays. On the surface, the play appears a sardonic, biting comedy, verging on farce, but the author intends us to penetrate beyond the comedy and to be aware of the true moral of this play, which is a tragic one.

The original title is difficult to translate. 'The Game of the Parties' would sound both clumsy and pedantic, so we have chosen to convey it with the now familiar *The Rules of the Game*. When the play first appeared in Milan in 1919, Marco Praga—himself a highly successful playwright—commented: 'One comedy was acted on the stage, and another in the auditorium. In the intervals, impassioned discussions took place between Pirandello's admirers and his enemies.'

This translation was first performed at the Arts Theatre in London, directed by John Fernald, assisted by the young Peter Hall. The major critics wrote thus of the play:

New Statesman and Nation (T. C. Worsley):
Pirandello's *The Rules of the Game* gave me such pleasure that I can write of it only in superlatives ... It is not so much the plot, neat as it is, that excites us; it is the superb condensation of the crackling dialogue from the very first. This is psychological drama played at a high stage of concentration.

Times Literary Supplement:
... a play whose biting wit puts to shame anything of native and

more recent vintage. It is the most extraordinary thing that we have had to remain for so long without theatrical experience of it ... Admirable comedy, so entertaining in itself, and so instructive in its implications.

Truth:
This play packs matter for a dozen dramas into its two hours ... Very funny indeed; some of the talk sparkles like Shaw at his best.

Observer (Kenneth Tynan):
In 'Il Giuoco delle Parti' translated by Robert Rietty and Noel Cregeen as *The Rules of the Game*, Pirandello created one of the few full length portraits of a Stoic in dramatic literature ... To object that it is bloodless is to miss the point; its very originality lies in its chill, analytical treatment of a problem which lesser playwrights would have solved in swamps of tears and regrets ... The play must be seen; it wears its thirty-seven years as if they were swaddling clothes.

Daily Sketch (Harold Conway):
The Arts Theatre came up last night with a novelty well-worth braving the snow and slush to see. Not only a novelty but a revelation—for *The Rules of the Game* shows that Pirandello could write a French farce with the best of them. An odd, ingeniously witty play, which saves its sting for the last five minutes.

Daily Express
The play has the brilliant cleverness of a painting by Picasso, which rearranges ordinary objects into fascinating jazz patterns. It takes a simple love triangle, but how Pirandello kicks it around! A play of dazzling wit.

Evening Standard (Milton Schulman):
Here is a scintillating mind juggling ideas with casual abandon. He can take a conventional romantic play and convert it into a dazzling display of intellectual pyrotechnics ... Bubbles over with symbolism and cynical argument.

The Stage:
Always several jumps ahead of his audience, Pirandello is able to stimulate, entertain, and frequently baffle those keen enough to follow his imperturbably witty course. With the lightest and most

disciplined of dramatic touches, he beats up his ideas with an intellectual egg-whisk until they spill frothily over his play. Chill and impersonal his treatment may be, but is none the less amusing and provocative.

Each in His Own Way ('Ciascuno a suo modo') first appeared in 1924. The play is a variation on the theme in *Six Characters in Search of an Author*. In the latter, he dwells on the contrast between the 'fixed reality of the literary characters and the ever changing reality of human beings.' The six characters are highly amused at the actors' attempt to portray them. In 'Ciascuno . . . ' the characters on the contrary, become passionately serious, recognising that their innermost thoughts are being expressed on the stage.

In both plays, Pirandello has deliberately turned the theatre—as we knew it then—inside out. It has been said of him that 'no other dramatist of this century has analized with such logical clearness the whole essence of theatrical illusion.'

Each in His Own Way ends in chaos and recriminations. In Pirandello's own words, 'Life obeys two forces which are opposed to each other and these two forces do not permit it to assume definite forms or to be forever fluid. If life moved eternally it could never acquire consistency. If it acquired consistency it would never move. And yet life must have both consistency and motion.'

Grafted ('L'Innesto') represents a change of approach by Pirandello. It is as though the playwright had turned his back on the cerebral gymnastics which typified his earlier attempts to show up our vices and follies with a biting and acrid humour, and decided to write in the idiom of the 'conventional well constructed' play where the characters express their pain in an easily recognisable form, and their passions are permitted to run their course in a more familiar manner.

Laura, brutally raped by a stranger while sketching in the gardens near her home, senses the stirrings of new life within her and longing for the experience of motherhood, hitherto denied her in seven years of an otherwise happy marriage, symbolically applies to herself the principles of grafting explained to her by a simple old gardener.

'If the plant is to bear fruit, the grafting must take place while the plant is in sap, otherwise the graft will never bind.' This leads her to convince herself that it matters little if the child is not from the actual seed of her husband, Giorgio; the important fact is that it was conceived while she was in love with him (in other words 'in sap') and therefore it is a child born of their love and as such has every right to be born.

Giorgio, absorbed in Victorian conventions and influenced by his meddling mother and the attitude of Italian society at large, insists on an abortion, but faced with her determination and his own fear of losing her, finally gives way and accepts her illusions. Her last triumphant cry 'My love has won' perhaps conceals Pirandello's cynical approach, for one is left asking oneself 'What in fact has she won?' *The Other Son* (L'Altro figlio) first appeared in 1923 and is one of the most powerful of Pirandello's dramas of peasant life in Sicily.

It starts with Maragrazia, an old peasant woman reduced to beggary, getting someone to write a letter for her to her two sons in Argentina, from whom she has not heard for many years.

Things are not so simple as they seem, and we make a series of puzzling discoveries. Firstly, Maragrazia's letters to her sons have never been properly written down or delivered. Secondly, she has another son who still lives in the village and is anxious to do his duty by her and give her a home. Thirdly, Maragrazia refuses to have anything to do with him. A young doctor who tries to help her goes further into the matter and unearths a horrifying story of ancient atrocity, continuing callousness and irretrievable estrangement.

The play ends with the tragic, imdomitable figure of Maragrazia composing yet another letter, this time with the help of the doctor, to her sons in Argentina.

ROBERT RIETTY

THE RULES OF THE GAME

Il giuoco delle parti

1918

Translated by
Robert Rietty and Noel Cregeen

CHARACTERS

LEONE GALA
SILIA GALA, Leone's wife
GUIDO VENANZI, Silia's lover
DOCTOR SPIGA
BARELLI
PHILIP, nicknamed 'Socrates', Leone's servant
MARQUIS MIGLIORITI
CLARA, Silia's maid
1st DRUNK
2nd DRUNK
3rd DRUNK
SEVERAL TENANTS, male and female

Scene : any town in Italy
Time : 1919

Note: the text has three drunks, but they can be reduced to two and the
lines distributed accordingly.

ACT I

The smartly furnished drawing-room of SILIA GALA's *flat.*
At the back, a large double sliding door, painted white, with red glass panes in the upper panels, divides this room from the dining-room. The front door and a window are on the left. In the right-hand wall there is a fireplace, and on the mantelpiece an ormolu clock. Near the fireplace, another door leads to a third room.
When the curtain rises, both sections of the glass door are slid right back into the wall. The time is about 10.15 pm.
GUIDO VENANZI, in evening dress, is standing by the dining-room table, on which a number of liqueur bottles can be seen in a silver stand.
SILIA GALA, in a light dressing-gown, is in the drawing-room, bunddled up day-dreaming in an armchair.

GUIDO: Chartreuse? (*He waits for an answer.* SILIA *ignores him.*) Anisette? (*Same result.*) Cognac? Well? Shall I choose? (*He pours out a glass of anisette, and takes it to* SILIA.) Here, try this.

SILIA *still takes no notice, and remains motionless for a few seconds. Then, shuddering with annoyance at finding him near her with the glass in his hand, she utters an exclamation of irritation.* GUIDO, *annoyed, drinks the glass in one gulp.*

GUIDO (*bowing*): Thanks for the trouble! I didn't really want it. (SILIA *resumes her original attitude.* GUIDO *puts down the glass, sits down, and turns to look at her.*) You might at least tell me what's the matter with you.

SILIA: If you imagine I'm here . . .

GUIDO: Oh, so you're not here? You're somewhere else, I suppose?

SILIA (*furiously*): Yes, I am somewhere else! Miles away.

GUIDO (*quietly, after a pause, as though to himself*): Then I'm alone, eh? In that case, I may as well see if there's anything worth stealing here. (*He gets up and pretends to search about the room.*) Let me see . . . a few paintings. N . . . no, too modern! Silver . . . hardly worth bothering about! (*He approaches* SILIA *as though he does not see her. When quite close to her he stops with an expression of mock surprise.*) Hullo! What's this? Your body left behind in the chair? I shall certainly take that! (*He tries to embrace her.*)

SILIA (*jumping to her feet and pushing him away*): Don't be so stupid! I've told you not to do that!

GUIDO: Pity! You're back again already! Your husband is right when he says our only real trips abroad are the ones we make in our imagination.

SILIA: That must be the fourth or fifth time you've mentioned **him** tonight.

GUIDO: It seems to be the only way of getting you to talk to me.

SILIA: No, Guido, it only makes you more of a bore.

GUIDO: Thanks!

SILIA (*after a long pause, with a sigh, distantly*): I saw it all so clearly!

GUIDO: What did you see?

SILIA: I must have read about it, I suppose. But everything was so clear and vivid. A woman, sitting there, smiling to herself as she worked.

GUIDO: What was she doing?

SILIA: I don't know—I couldn't see her hands. But it was something women do while their men are away fishing. I think it's in Iceland. Yes, that's where it is.

GUIDO: You were dreaming you were in . . . Iceland?

SILIA: Yes, I was day-dreaming. But that's the way I always travel. (*Pause*) It's got to stop! It's got to stop! (*Aggressively*) This can't go on any longer.

GUIDO: Meaning me?

SILIA: No. Me.

GUIDO: But don't you see that anything that concerns you concerns me too?

SILIA (*annoyed*): Oh, God! You always see everything on such a tiny scale. You're shut up in a smug little cut and dried world of your own, where nothing is allowed to exist that doesn't concern you personally. I bet geography still means nothing more to you than a textbook, and a map on a school-room wall!

GUIDO (*puzzled*): Geography?

SILIA: Yes. Didn't your teacher set you lists of names to be learnt by heart for homework?

GUIDO: Lord, yes! What a bore!

SILIA: But rivers, mountains, countries, islands, continents—they really **do** exist, you know.

GUIDO (*sarcastically*): Really? Thanks for telling me!

SILIA: And there are people living there—and all the time we're cooped up in this room.

GUIDO (*as though light had suddenly dawned on him*): Ah, I see. You're hinting that I ought to take you abroad.

SILIA: There you go again! I make a perfectly general statement, and you immediately think it must have some bearing on our situation. I'm not hinting at anything. I'm merely trying to broaden your outlook. I can't bear this life any longer. I'm stifled!

GUIDO: But what sort of life **do** you want?

SILIA: I don't know. Any life that's different from this! God, if I could only see the faintest glimmer of hope for the future! I tell you I'd be perfectly happy just basking in that ray of hope—without running to flatten my nose against the window-pane to see what there is in store for me outside.

GUIDO: You're talking as if you were in prison!

SILIA: I am in prison!

GUIDO: Oh? And who's keeping you there?

SILIA: You, and everyone else! Even my own body, because I can never forget that it's a woman's. How can I, when you men are always staring at my figure? I never think about my

body until I catch men's eyes ogling. Often I burst out laughing. 'Well,' I say to myself, 'there's no getting away from
it—I **am** a woman!'

GUIDO: I don't think you've any reason to complain about
that.

SILIA: Because I'm attractive? (*Pause*) But can't you see that
all **this** is mainly due to my being continually reminded I'm
a woman, and forced to be one when I don't want to be?

GUIDO (*slowly, detached*): Like tonight, for example.

SILIA: Being a woman has never given **me** any pleasure.

GUIDO: Not even the pleasure of making a man miserable?

SILIA: Yes, **that** perhaps. Often.

GUIDO (*as before*): Tonight, for example. (*Pause. SILIA sits,
absorbed.*)

SILIA (*fretfully*): But one's own life! . . . The life we don't
share with anybody—not even ourselves . . .

GUIDO: What **are** you talking about?

SILIA: Have you never stood gazing at your reflection in a
mirror, without thinking about yourself? Suddenly you feel
that your face belongs to someone else, a stranger, and you
study it intently. Then you see a stray lock of hair or something—automatically you push it back into place, and immediately the spell is broken, everything is spoilt.

GUIDO: And so . . . ?

SILIA: Other people's eyes are like a mirror. So are our own,
when we are using them to look at ourselves to find out the
way we ought to live; the way we are bound to live, in fact.
Oh, I can't explain! (*Pause.*)

GUIDO (*approaching*): Shall I tell you frankly why you're
getting so worked up?

SILIA (*promptly*): Because you're here—standing in front of me!

GUIDO (*taking it to heart*): Oh! In that case would you like me
to go?

SILIA: Yes, you had better.

GUIDO: But why, Silia? (SILIA *shrugs her shoulders.*) Why
do you treat me so badly?

SILIA: I'm not treating you badly. I don't want people to see
you here too often, that's all.

GUIDO: Too often! Why, I hardly ever come here. It must be more than a week since I was here last. Obviously, time passes too quickly for you.

SILIA: Quickly? Every day seems an eternity!

GUIDO (*close*): Then why do you still pretend that I count for nothing in your life? Silia . . . (*He tries to embrace her.*)

SILIA (*irritated*): Oh, Guido, for heaven's sake!

GUIDO: I've waited for you day after day. You hardly let me see you any more . . .

SILIA: But can't you see the state I'm in?

GUIDO: That's simply because you don't know what you want. You go and invoke some vague hope or other that will open a chink for you into the future.

SILIA: According to you, I suppose I ought to go forward to meet the future with a ruler in my hand to measure all my desires. 'So much I may allow myself to want, and no more.' Like doling out sweets to a child!

GUIDO: I expect you think I'm being pedantic!

SILIA: Yes, I do. All that you've been saying bores me stiff!

GUIDO: Thanks!

SILIA: You want to make me believe that I have had everything I could wish for, and that I'm getting 'worked-up' like this now—as you put it—because I'm snatching at something out of reach, at the impossible. Isn't that it? (*Mimicking him.*) 'It's not reasonable!' Oh, I know that! But what would you have me do? I **do** want the impossible!

GUIDO: What, for instance?

SILIA: Can you tell me what I've had out of life to make me happy?

GUIDO: Happiness is all a question of degree. One person is satisfied with little; another has everything, and is never satisfied.

SILIA: Do you imagine I have everything?

GUIDO: No, but you're never content with things as they are. What on earth **are** you hankering after?

SILIA (*as though to herself*): I want to be rich . . . my own mistress . . . free! (*Suddenly flaring up.*) Haven't you understood yet that all this has been **his** revenge?

GUIDO: It's your own fault! You don't know how to use the freedom he's given you.

SILIA: Freedom to let myself be made love to by you or any other man; freedom to stay here or go anywhere I please . . . Oh, yes! I'm free! Free as air . . . But what if I'm never myself?

GUIDO: What do you mean, never yourself?

SILIA: Do you really think I'm free to be myself and do just as I like, as though no one else were there to prevent me?

GUIDO: Well, who is preventing you?

SILIA: **He** is! Throwing this precious freedom at me like an old shoe, and going off to live by himself—after spending three years proving to me that this wonderful freedom has no real existence. No matter what use I try to make of it, I shall always be his slave! Even a slave of that chair of his! Look at it: standing in front of me determined to be one of **his** chairs, not something belonging to **me**, and made for **me** to sit in!

GUIDO: This is an obsession!

SILIA: That man haunts me!

GUIDO: But you hardly ever see him!

SILIA: But he's there, he exists, and I shall always be haunted by him as long as I know he exists. Dear God, I wish he were dead!

GUIDO: Well, he practically is dead as far as you're concerned. He's stopped paying you those absurd visits in the evenings, hasn't he?

SILIA: Yes . . . Now he comes as far as the front door and sends the maid up to ask if I have any message for him.

GUIDO: Well, is that so terrible?

SILIA: Of course! Because he **ought** to come up to the flat and stay for half an hour every evening. That's what we agreed he was to do.

GUIDO: Really, Silia! You just said you were haunted by him, and now . . .

SILIA: Don't you see it's the fact of his being alive, his mere existence that haunts me? It's not his body at all. On the contrary; it would be much better if I did see him. And it's just because he knows that, he doesn't let me see him any more. If he did come in and sit down in that chair over there, he'd seem like any other man, neither uglier nor better-looking. I'd see those eyes of his that I never liked—God, they're horrible. Sharp as needles and vacant at the same time. I'd hear that voice of his that gets on my nerves. I'd have something tangible to grapple with—and I'd even get some satisfaction out of giving him the bother of coming upstairs for nothing!

GUIDO: I don't believe it.

SILIA: What don't you believe?

GUIDO: That anything could possibly bother him!

SILIA: Yes, that's the trouble! He's like a ghost, quite detached from life, existing only to haunt other people's lives. I sit for hours on end absolutely crushed by the thought. There he is, alone in his own apartment, dressed up as a cook—dressed up as a cook, I ask you!—looking down on everybody from above, watching and understanding every move you make, everything you do, knowing all your thoughts, and making you foresee exactly what you're going to do next—and, of course, when you know what it is, you no longer want to do it! That man has paralysed me! I've only one idea continually gnawing at my brain: how to get rid of him, how to free myself from him. (*The telephone rings offstage.*)

GUIDO: Really, Silia, aren't you being rather melodramatic!

SILIA: It's the truth. (*There is a knock at the door on the left.*) Come in.

CLARA (*opens the door*): Excuse me, Signora, the master has rung up from downstairs.

SILIA: Ah, so he's here!

CLARA: He wants to know if there's any message.

SILIA: Yes, there is. Tell him to come up, Clara.

GUIDO: But, Silia . . .

SILIA: Tell him to come up.

CLARA: Very good, Signora. (*She goes.*)

GUIDO: But why, Silia? Why tonight when I'm here?

SILIA: For the very reason that you are here!

GUIDO: No, Silia—don't do it.

SILIA: Yes, I shall—to punish you for coming. What's more I'll leave you here to deal with him. I'm going to bed. (*She goes towards the door on the right.*)

GUIDO (*running after her and holding her back*): No, don't Silia! Are you mad? What will he say?

SILIA: What do you expect him to say?

GUIDO: Silia . . . listen . . . it's late . . .

SILIA: So much the better.

GUIDO: No, no, Silia. That would be going too far. It's madness.

SILIA (*freeing herself from him*): I don't wish to see him.

GUIDO: Neither do I.

SILIA: You're going to entertain him.

GUIDO: Oh, no, I'm not. He won't find me here either. (SILIA *goes into her room.* GUIDO *immediately runs into the dining-room, shutting the glass door. There is a knock at the front door.*)

LEONE (*off*): May I come in? (*He opens the door and puts his head round.*) May I? . . . (*He breaks off, seeing no one there.*) Well . . . well . . .

He looks round the room, then takes his watch out of his pocket, goes to the mantelpiece, opens the face of the clock and moves the hand so that it strikes twice, then puts his watch back in his pocket and settles down calmly to await the passing of the agreed half hour.

After a short pause a confused whispering is heard from the dining-room. It is SILIA *trying to urge* GUIDO *into the drawing-room.* LEONE *remains motionless. Presently, one section of the glass door opens and* GUIDO *enters, leaving the door open.*

GUIDO (*ill at ease*): Oh . . . hullo, Leone. I dropped in for a spot of chartreuse.

LEONE: At half past ten?

GUIDO: Yes . . . As a matter of fact . . . I was just going.

LEONE: I didn't mean that. Was it green chartreuse or yellow?

GUIDO: Oh, I . . . I don't remember. Green, I think.

LEONE: At about two o'clock you'll have the most horrible

nightmare, and wake up with your tongue feeling like a loofah.

GUIDO (*shuddering*): Oh, don't say that!

LEONE: Yes, you will—result of drinking liqueurs on an empty stomach. Where's Silia?

GUIDO (*embarrassed*): Well, er . . . She was in there, with me.

LEONE: Where is she now?

GUIDO: I don't know. She . . . she sent me in here when she heard you had come. I expect she'll be . . . joining you soon.

LEONE: Is there something she wants to say to me?

GUIDO: N-no . . . I . . . don't think so.

LEONE: Then why did she make me come up?

GUIDO: Well, I was just saying good-bye, when the maid came in and told her you'd rung up from the hall . . .

LEONE: As I do every evening.

GUIDO: Yes, but . . . apparently she wanted you to come up.

LEONE: Did she say so?

GUIDO: Oh, yes, she said so.

LEONE: Is she angry?

GUIDO: A bit, yes, because . . . I believe that . . . Well, I think you two agreed, didn't you? . . . For the sake of appearances . . .

LEONE: You can leave out the appearances!

GUIDO: I mean, to avoid scandal . . .

LEONE: Scandal?

GUIDO: . . . without going to court.

LEONE: Waste of time!

GUIDO: Well, without openly quarrelling then—you separated.

LEONE: But who on earth would ever quarrel with me? I always give way to everybody.

GUIDO: True. In fact, that's one of your most enviable qualities. But—if I may say so—you go rather too far.

LEONE: You think so?

GUIDO: Yes, because, you see, so often you . . . (*He looks at him and breaks off.*)

LEONE: Well?

GUIDO: You upset people.

LEONE (*amused*): No! Really? How?

GUIDO: Because ... you always follow their suggestions. You always do what other people want. I bet that when your wife said to you 'Let's have a judicial separation', you answered ...

LEONE: 'Very well, let's have a judicial separation.'

GUIDO: There you are, you see! And then when she changed her mind because she didn't want any bother with lawyers and suggested you separate merely by mutual agreement ...

LEONE: I replied, 'All right, if that's the way you want it, we'll separate by mutual agreement.' I even went away and left her the apartment. I told her she could alter anything she liked, redecorate the place, refurnish it to her own taste ... The only thing I insisted on was that she keep my clock—which she always forgets to wind, bless her—and my favourite armchair, so I can feel a little bit at home on these half hour visits. What more could she want?

GUIDO: That's all very well, but if she came to you and said, 'We can't go on quarrelling like this' ...

LEONE: ... I should have said 'Well then, my dear, we'll not quarrel any more. We'll forget there was ever a difference between us, and start our life together afresh.'

GUIDO: But don't you see that all this is bound to upset people? One gets in the way of behaving as though you didn't exist, and then ... How can I explain it? However one tries to ignore your existence, sooner or later, one gets to a point where one can't go any further. It's a dead end, and one stands there bewildered, because ... Well, it's no use, you **do** exist!

LEONE: Undoubtedly. (*He smiles.*) I exist. (*In a rather sharper tone.*) Ought I **not** to exist?

GUIDO: No, good God, I didn't mean that.

LEONE: But you're right, my dear chap! I ought not to exist. I assure you I do my utmost to exist as little as possible—for my own sake as well as others! But what can you do? The fault lies with the fact: **I am alive**. And when a fact has happened, it stands there, like a prison, shutting you in. I married Silia, or to be more precise, I let her marry me. Voilà:

another fact! Almost immediately after our wedding, she began to fume and fret, and twist and turn, in her frantic efforts to escape, and I . . . I tell you Guido, it caused me a great deal of unhappiness. In the end we hit upon this solution. I left her everything here, taking away with me only my books and my pots and pans, which, as you know, are quite indispensable to me. But I realise it's useless, because—in name, anyway—the 'part' assigned to me by a fact which cannot be destroyed, remains. I am her husband. That, too, perhaps ought occasionally to be borne in mind! (*He pauses. GUIDO* looks a little uncomfortable. Suddenly.) You know what blind people are like, don't you, Venanzi?

GUIDO: Blind people?

LEONE: They are never 'alongside' things, if you follow me.

GUIDO: I don't.

LEONE: If you see a blind man groping for something, and you try to help him by saying 'there it is, just beside you,' what does he do? He immediately turns and faces you. It's the same with that dear woman. She's never by your side—always facing you, opposed to you. (*He pauses, glancing towards the glass door.*) It looks as if my wife isn't coming in. (*He takes his watch out of his pocket, sees that the half-hour is not yet up and puts it back.*)

LEONE: You don't know what it was she wanted to say to me?

GUIDO: I . . . don't think there was anything . . . really.

LEONE: In that case, all she wanted was **this**. (*He makes a gesture signifying 'you and me.'*)

GUIDO (*puzzled*): I don't follow.

LEONE: This situation, my dear chap. She wanted to have the satisfaction of forcing us two to meet like this, face to face.

GUIDO: Perhaps she thinks that I . . .

LEONE: . . . have already gone? No, she would have come in.

GUIDO (*getting ready to go*): Oh, well, in that case . . .

LEONE (*quickly, detaining him*): Oh, no, please don't go. I shall be leaving in a few minutes. (*He rises.*) Ah, Venanzi, it's a sad thing when one has learnt every move in the game.

GUIDO: What game?

LEONE: Why . . . this one. The whole game—of life.

GUIDO: Have you learnt it?

LEONE: Yes, a long time ago. And the way to come through it unscathed.

GUIDO: I wish you'd teach me how to do that.

LEONE: Oh, my dear Venanzi, it wouldn't be of any use to you! To get through safe and sound you must know how to defend yourself. But it's a kind of defence that you, probably, wouldn't be able to understand. How shall I describe it? A desperate one.

GUIDO: How do you mean, desperate? Rash? Reckless?

LEONE: Oh no, not that at all. I mean desperate in its literal sense. Absolutely hopeless—but without the faintest shadow of bitterness, for all that.

GUIDO: Well, what is this defence?

LEONE: It's the firmest and most unshakeable of all defences. You see, when there's no more hope left, you're not tempted to make even the slightest concession, either to others or to yourself.

GUIDO: It doesn't sound like a defence to me—but, if it is, what are you defending?

LEONE (*looks at him severely and darkly for a moment: then, controlling himself, he sinks back into an impenetrable serenity*): The Nothing that lies inside yourself. That is, if you succeed, as I have done, in achieving this nothingness within you. What do you imagine you should defend? Defend yourself, I tell you, against the injuries life inevitably inflicts upon us all; I have injured myself, through Silia, for so many years. I am injuring her now, even though I isolate her from myself completely. You are injuring me . . .

GUIDO: I?

LEONE: Of course—inevitably! (*Looking into his eyes.*) Surely you don't imagine you are **not** doing me any injury.

GUIDO: Well . . . (*He pales.*) I'm not aware . . .

LEONE (*encouragingly*): Oh, unconsciously, my dear Venanzi, quite unconsciously. When you sit down to eat a roast chicken or a tender veal cutlet, do you ever consider who provides your meal? Are you consciously aware that the morsel impaled on your fork was once a living, breathing, feeling creature? No, you never think about it. Make no mistake, we all injure each other—and each man injures himself too, naturally! That's life! There's only one thing to do—empty yourself.

GUIDO: Oh, fine! And what's left then?

LEONE: The satisfaction, not of living for yourself any more, but of watching others live—and even of watching yourself, from outside, living that little part of life you are still bound to live.

GUIDO: Only too little, alas!

LEONE: Yes, but you get a marvellous compensation—the thrill of the intellectual game that clears away all the sentimental sediment from your mind, and fixes in calm, precise orbits all that moves tumultuously within you. But the enjoyment of this clear, calm vacuum that you create within you may be dangerous, because, among other things, you run the risk of going up among the clouds like a balloon, unless you put inside yourself the necessary measure of ballast.

GUIDO: Oh, I see! By eating well?

LEONE (*ignoring the interjection*): To re-establish your equilibrium, so that you will always stay upright. You know those celluloid toys?—those funny little hollow figures you give to children to play with? You can knock them over any way you like, and they always spring up again. That's because of their lead counter-weight. I assure you we're very much the same as they are. Only you have to learn how to make yourself hollow, and—more important—how to provide yourself with a counterweight.

GUIDO: I don't follow you.

LEONE: I feared you wouldn't.

GUIDO (*hastily*): I'm not really unintelligent, you know, but . . .

LEONE: An anchor then? Does that make sense to you? A ship riding at anchor in a storm? Find yourself an anchor, then, my dear Venanzi—some hobby, some absorbing mental occupation, some fanciful conceit—then you'll be safe.

GUIDO: Oh, no, no! Thanks very much! That sort of thing is not for me. It sounds much too difficult.

LEONE: It's not easy, I grant you, because you can't buy these anchors ready made. You have to make them for yourself—

and not just one, either. You need many anchors, one to suit each emergency, every incident in life. And, too, they must be stout and strong, to stand the strain of any violent incident that may burst upon you without warning.

GUIDO: Yes, but surely there are certain unforeseen incidents, sometimes really shattering ones, that even you can't . . .

LEONE: That's just where my cooking comes in. It's wonderful what storms you can weather if you're a good cook.

GUIDO: What kind of storms? Domestic, do you mean?

LEONE: Any storm. Any emergency. After all, it is never the emergency itself which you have to fear, but its effect upon you.

GUIDO: But that in itself can be quite terrible.

LEONE: But more or less terrible according to the person who experiences it. That's why I say you must defend yourself against yourself—against the feelings immediately aroused in you by anything that happens to you. Your own feelings— they are the weapons which an incident uses in its attack upon you.

GUIDO: But I can't defend myself against my own feelings.

LEONE: Oh, you can. Counter-attack, my dear fellow. You must grapple with the incident without hesitation, before it gets a chance to engage your feelings, and get out of it anything that may be of advantage to you. The residue will be powerless to injure you, you can laugh at it, play with it, make it the fanciful conceit I mentioned just now.

GUIDO (*more and more bewildered*): I'm afraid I still don't quite . . .

LEONE: Look, Venanzi. Imagine for a moment that you notice an egg suddenly hurtling through the air straight towards you . . .

GUIDO: . . . an egg?

LEONE: Yes, an egg. A fresh one. It doesn't matter who has thrown it, or where it comes from; that's beside the point.

GUIDO: But suppose it turns out to be a bullet and not an egg?

LEONE (*smiling*): Then it's too late to think about emptying yourself. The bullet will do the job for you, and that's the end of the matter.

GUIDO: All right—let's stick to your egg; although what a fresh egg has to do with the matter, I'm blessed if I can see.

LEONE: To give you a fresh image of events and ideas. Well, now, if you're not prepared to catch the egg, what happens? Either you stand still and the egg hits you and smashes, or you duck and it misses you and smashes on the ground. In either case the result is a wasted egg. But if you are prepared, you catch it, and then—why there's no end to what you can do with it, if you're a good cook. You can boil it, or poach it, or fry it, or make an omelette of it. Or you can simply pierce it at each end and suck out the yoke. What's left in your hand then?

GUIDO: The empty shell.

LEONE: Exactly. That empty shell is your fanciful conceit. You can amuse yourself with it by sticking it on a pin and making it spin; or you can toss it from one hand to the other like a ping-pong ball. When you're tired of playing with it, what do you do? You crush it in your hand and throw it away. (*At this point* SILIA, *in the dining-room, suddenly laughs loudly.*)

SILIA (*hiding behind the closed section of the glass door*): But I'm not an empty egg shell in your hand.

LEONE (*turning quickly and going to the door*): No, dear. And you no longer come through the air towards **me** for **me** to catch. (*He has hardly finished saying this when* SILIA, *without showing herself, shuts the other half-door in his face.* LEONE *stands there for a moment, nodding. Then he comes forward again and turns to* GUIDO.) That's a great misfortune for me, my dear Venanzi. She was a wonderful school of experience. I've come to miss her. She is full of unhappiness because she's full of life. Not one life only, many. But there isn't one of them that will ever give her an anchor. There's no salvation for her. (*Pointedly*) And so there's no peace . . . either for her, or with her. (GUIDO, *absorbed in thought, unconsciously nods too, with a sad expression on his face.*) You agree?

GUIDO (*thoughtfully*): Yes . . . it's perfectly true.

LEONE: You're probably unaware of all the riches there are in her . . . qualities of mind and spirit you would never believe to be hers—because you know only one facet of her character, from which you have built up your idea of what is for you, and always will be, the real and only Silia. You wouldn't think it possible, for example, for Silia to go about her housework some mornings carefree, relaxed, happily singing or humming to herself. But she does, you know. I used to hear her sometimes, going from room to room singing in a sweet little quavering voice, like a child's. A different woman, I'm not saying that just for the sake of saying it. Really a different woman—without knowing it! For a few moments when she is out of herself, she is just a child, singing. And if you could see how she sits sometimes, absorbed, gazing into space; a distant, living glow reflected in her eyes, and unconsciously smoothing her hair with idly straying fingers. Who is she then? Not the Silia you know—another Silia, a Silia that can't live because she is unknown to herself, since no one has ever said to her 'I love you when you are like that; that's the way I want you always to be.'

If you told her that, she'd ask you, 'How do you want me to be?' You would reply 'As you were just now.' Then she would turn to you, 'What was I like,' she would say, 'what was I doing?' 'You were singing.' 'I was singing?' 'Yes, and you were smoothing your hair like this.' She would not know it.

She would tell you it wasn't true. She positively would not recognise herself in your picture of her as you had just seen her—if you **could** see her like that, for you always see only one side of her! How sad it is, Guido! Here's a sweet, gracious potentiality of a life she might have—and she hasn't got it! (*A sad pause. In the silence, the ormolu clock strikes eleven.*) Ah, eleven o'clock. Say good-night to her from me.

SILIA (*quickly opening the glass door*): Wait—wait a moment.

LEONE: Oh, no. Time's up.

SILIA: I wanted to give you this. (*She puts an egg shell into his hand, laughing.*)

LEONE: Oh, but **I** haven't sucked it! Here . . . *He goes quickly to* GUIDO *and gives him the egg shell.*) Let's give it to Guido! (GUIDO *automatically takes the egg shell and stands stupidly with it in his hand, while* LEONE, *laughing loudly, goes off through the door on the left.*)

SILIA: I'd give anything for someone to kill him!

GUIDO: I'd love to chuck this egg at his head. (*He runs towards the window on the left.*)

SILIA (*laughing*): Here, give it to me! I'll throw it at him from the window. (GUIDO *gives her the egg shell, or rather, lets her take it from him.*)

GUIDO: Will you be able to hit him?

SILIA: Yes, as he comes out of the front door. (*She leans out of the window, looking down, ready to throw the egg shell.*)

GUIDO (*behind her*): Careful. (SILIA *throws the shell, then suddenly draws back with an exclamation of dismay.*) What have you done?

SILIA: Oh, Lord!

GUIDO: Did you hit someone else?

SILIA: Yes. The wind made it swerve.

GUIDO: Naturally! It was empty. Trust a woman not to allow for the wind!

SILIA: They are coming up.

GUIDO: Who's coming up?

SILIA: There were four men talking by the door. They were coming in just as he went out. Perhaps they are tenants.

GUIDO: Well, what does it matter, anyway? (*He takes advantage of her consternation and kisses her.*)

SILIA: It looks as though it landed on one of them.

GUIDO: But an empty egg shell couldn't possibly hurt him! Forget about it! (*Recalling* Leone's *words, but passionately and without caricature.*) You know, darling, you are just like a child.

SILIA: What **are** you saying?

GUIDO: You are like a child tonight, and I love you when you're like that. That's the way I want you always to be.

SILIA (*laughs*): You're repeating what **he** said.

GUIDO (*not put off by her laughter, but is still passionate, his desire increasing*): Yes, I know I am, but it's true, it's true! Can't you see you're just a wayward child?

SILIA: A child? (*Raising her hands to his face, as though to scratch him.*) More likely a tigress!

GUIDO (*without letting her go*): For him, perhaps, but not for me. I love you so. To me you're a child.

SILIA (*half laughing*): All right, then, you kill him for me!

GUIDO: Oh, darling, do be serious.

SILIA: Well, if I'm a child I can ask you to do that for me, can't I?

GUIDO (*playing up*): Because he's your 'bogeyman'?

SILIA: Yes, he's the 'bogeyman' who makes me so frightened. Will you kill him for me?

GUIDO: Yes, yes, I'll kill him ... but not now, later. Now I want to ... (*He clasps her more closely.*)

SILIA (*struggling*): No, no! Guido, please ...

GUIDO: Oh, Silia, you must know how much I love you; how I long for you!

SILIA (*as before, but languidly*): No. I tell you.

GUIDO (*trying to lead her towards the door on the right*): Yes, yes! Come, Silia.

SILIA: No. please! Leave me!

GUIDO: How can I leave you now, darling?

SILIA: No, Guido, no! Not in the flat! I shouldn't like the maid to ... (*There is a knock on the door, left.*) There, you see?

GUIDO: Don't let her in. I'll wait for you in your room. (*He goes towards the door on the right.*) But don't be long. (*He leaves, shutting the door.* SILIA *goes to the other door, but before she reaches it,* CLARA *is heard shouting outside.*)

CLARA: Take your hands off me. Go away! She doesn't live here! (*The door bursts open and* MARQUIS MIGLIORITI *enters with three other 'young-men-about-town', all in evening dress. They are very drunk, very high spirited, and very determined to enter.*)

MIGLIORITI: Out of the way, you old owl. What do you mean by saying she doesn't live here, when she's here all the time.

1st DRUNK: Lovely Pepita! The gay senorita!

2nd DRUNK: Viva Espana. Viva Espana.

3rd DRUNK (*not so stupidly drunk as the others*): I say, fellows. Just look at this flat! *C'est tout a fait charmant!*

SILIA (*to* CLARA): What's the meaning of this? Who are they? How did they get in?

CLARA: They forced their way in, Signora. They're drunk.

MIGLIORITI (*to* CLARA): Some force, eh! You old owl!

1st DRUNK: Some drunks!

2nd DRUNK: Georgeously drunk drunks!

MIGLIORITI (*to* SILIA): But you invited me, Senorita! You dropped an egg shell on me from the window!

2nd DRUNK: D'you know what we are? We are four gentlemen!

1st DRUNK: Caballeros!

3rd DRUNK (*pointing to the dining-room and then going into it*): I wonder if a client gets a drink here? (*He notices the decanters on the table.*) Ah, we're in luck! *C'est tout a fait delicieux!*

SILIA (*noting the implications of the word 'client'*): Good Lord! What do they want?

CLARA (*to* MIGLIORITI): How dare you! This is a respectable house!

MIGLIORITI: But of course, we know that. (*To* SILIA.) Charming Pepita!

SILIA: Pepita!?

CLARA: Yes, Signora ... that woman next door. I kept telling them this wasn't her flat. (SILIA *bursts out laughing. Then a sinister light comes into her eyes, as though a diabolical idea has come into her head.*)

SILIA: Why yes, of course, gentlemen, I am Pepita.

2nd DRUNK: Viva Espana. Viva Pepita!

SILIA (*to all three*): Do sit down, won't you? Or perhaps you'd rather join your friend in there for a drink?

MIGLIORITI (*attempting to kiss her*): No, I ... well, really ... I'd rather ...

SILIA (*evades him*): Rather what?

MIGLIORITI: I'd rather drink **you** first!

SILIA: Wait! Wait a moment!

2nd DRUNK (*imitating* MIGLIORITI's *actions*): Me too, Pepita!

SILIA (*warding him off*): You too? All right ... steady now.

2nd DRUNK: What we want is an ab-sho-lutely Spanish night!

1st DRUNK: Personally, I don't actually propose to do any thing, but ...

SILIA: Yes, all right . . . all right . . . steady now. Now come and sit down over here, boys. (*She frees herself and pushes them towards chairs, making them sit down.*) That's right . . . fine! That's it. (*They mutter among themselves.* SILIA *runs to* CLARA *and whispers.*)

SILIA: Go upstairs and fetch some of the neighbours. Downstairs too. Hurry! (CLARA *nods and runs off.* GUIDO *starts to open the bedroom door.*)

SILIA (*to* MIGLIORITI *and the others*): Excuse me a minute . . . (*She goes to the door on the right and locks it to prevent* GUIDO *from coming in.*)

MIGLIORITI (*rising unsteadily*): Oh, if you've got a gentleman in there already, carry on you know, don't mind us!

2nd DRUNK: No, don't mind us, carry on—carry on—we don't mind waiting.

1st DRUNK: Personally, I don't actually propose to do anything but . . . (*He tries to get up.*)

SILIA (*to* MIGLIORITI *and the* 1st DRUNK): Don't get up! Stay where you are. (*To all three.*) Listen—you gentlemen are quite . . . I mean, you know what you are doing, don't you?

ALL: Of course! Absolutely. Of course we do. Why shouldn't we? Know what we're doing, indeed!

SILIA: And you don't for a moment suspect that you are in a respectable house, do you?

3rd DRUNK (*staggering in from the dining-room with a glass in his hand*): Oh, *oui . . . mais . . . n'exagere pas, mon petit chou! Nous voulons nous amuser un peu . . . Voilà tout*, my little cabbage!

SILIA: But your little cabbage is at home only to friends. Now, if you want to be friends . . .

2nd DRUNK: *Mais certainement*!

1st DRUNK: Intimate friends! (*He tries to rise and bow, then subsides, muttering* 'Dear little Pepita!' 'Lovely little Pepita!' *etc.*)

SILIA: Then please tell me your names.

2nd DRUNK: My name is Coco.

SILIA: No . . . not like that . . .

2nd DRUNK: Honestly, my name is Coco.

1st DRUNK: And mine is Meme.

SILIA: No, no! I mean, will you give me your visiting cards?

2nd DRUNK: Oh no, no, no! Thank you very much, swee-theart.

1st DRUNK: I haven't got one . . . I've lost my wallet . . . (*To* MIGLIORITI.) Be a good chap, and give her one for me.

SILIA (*sweetly—to* MIGLIORITI): Yes, you're the nicest. You'll give me yours, won't you?

MIGLIORITI (*taking out his wallet*): Certainly. I have no objection.

2nd DRUNK: He can give you cards for all of us . . . *Voilà!*

MIGLIORITI: Here you are, Pepita.

SILIA: Oh thank you. Good. (*She reads it.*) So you are Marquis Miglioriti?

1st DRUNK (*laughing*): That's right—he's a Marquis . . . But only a little one!

SILIA (*to* 2nd DRUNK): And you are Meme?

1st DRUNK: No, I'm Meme. (*Pointing to* 2nd DRUNK.) He's Coco.

SILIA: Oh yes, of course. Coco—Meme (*To the* 3rd DRUNK.) And you?

3rd DRUNK (*with a silly, sly look*): *Moi? Moi . . . Je ne sais pas, mon petit chou.*

SILIA: Well, it doesn't matter. One is enough.

2nd DRUNK: But we all want to be in it. We all want . . .

3rd DRUNK: . . . an absolutely Spanish night!

1st DRUNK: Personally, I don't actually propose to do anything, but I should love to see you dance, Pepita . . . You know, with castanets . . . Ta trrrra ti ta ti, ta trrra ti ta ti . . . (*He breaks into 'Habanera' from the opera Carmen.*)

2nd DRUNK: Yes, yes. Dance first . . . And **then** . . .

MIGLIORITI: But not dressed like that!

3rd DRUNK: Why dressed at all, gentlemen?

2nd DRUNK (*rising and staggering up to* SILIA): Yes, that's right! Without a stitch! (MIGLIORITI *and the others crowd round* SILIA *as if to strip her.*)

ALL: Yes, stripped . . . in the altogether. That's the idea! Splendid! Without a stitch. Splendid!

SILIA (*freeing herself*): But not in here, gentlemen, please. Naked, if you like. But not here.

3rd DRUNK: Where then?

SILIA: Down in the square.

MIGLIORITI (*very still, sobering up a little*): In the square?

1st DRUNK (*quietly*): Naked in the square?

SILIA: Of course! Why not? It's the ideal place. The moon is shining—there won't be anyone about . . . just the statue of the king on horseback. And you four gentlemen . . . in evening dress. (*At this point tenants of the floors above and below rush in with* CLARA, *shouting confusedly. One elderly gentleman holds a little riding crop in his hand as a weapon.*)

THE TENANTS: What's the matter? What's happened? Who are they? What's going on here? What have they done to her? Has she been assaulted?

CLARA: There they are! There they are!

SILIA (*suddenly changing her tone and demeanour*): I've been assaulted! Assaulted in my own home! They forced their way in, knocked me down, and pulled me about, as you can see. They've molested me and insulted me in every possible way, the cowards!

A TENANT (*trying to chase them out*): Get out of here! Get out!

A TENANT: Stand back! Leave her alone!

A TENANT: Come along! Get out of here.

1st DRUNK: All right! Keep calm! Keep calm!

A TENANT: Go on! Get out!

A WOMAN TENANT: What scoundrels.

MIGLIORITI: Well, this is an open house isn't it? Anybody can come in, surely?

1st DRUNK: Spain is doing a brisk trade!

A WOMAN TENANT: Well . . . Really!!!

A WOMAN TENANT: Get out, you disgusting drunken lot, you!

3rd DRUNK: Oh, I say, there's no need to make such a fuss, you know.

MIGLIORITI: Dear Pepita . . .

A TENANT: Pepita?

A WOMAN TENANT: Pepita! This isn't Pepita, young man. This is Signora Gala.

A TENANT: Of course. Signora Gala.

MIGLIORITI & THE 3 DRUNKS: Signora Gala.

3rd DRUNK: No Pepita?

A TENANT: Certainly not! Signora Gala.

A WOMAN TENANT: You ought to be ashamed of yourselves. Good for nothing, drunken hooligans, that's what you are!

2nd DRUNK: Oh, well . . . In that case, we'll apologise to the Signora for our mistake.

ALL THE TENANTS: Go along now! Get out! Leave this place at once!

1st DRUNK: *Doucement . . . doucement, s'il vous plait!*

2nd DRUNK: We thought she was Pepita.

3rd DRUNK: Yes, and we wanted to do homage to Spain. To-reador, tum, tum-ti, tumti, tummm . . . (*He starts to sing 'Habanera' again.*)

A TENANT: That's quite enough, now! Get out!

2nd DRUNK: No! First we must beg the Signora's pardon.

A TENANT: Stop it. That'll do now. Go home.

MIGLIORITI: Yes—very well. But, look here, all of you, look here. (*He kneels in front of* SILIA.) Down on our knees, we offer you our humble apologies.

ALL DRUNKS: That's right . . . on our knees. Go on, Coco . . . down you go . . . etc.

SILIA: Oh, no! That's not good enough. Marquis, I have your name, and you and your friends will have to answer for the outrage you have done to me in my own home.

MIGLIORITI: But, Signora—if we beg your pardon . . .

SILIA: I accept no apologies.

MIGLIORITI (*rising, much sobered*): Very well. You have my card . . . and I'm quite ready to answer—

SILIA: Now get out of my flat—at once! (*The* FOUR DRUNKS, *who nevertheless feel compelled to bow, are driven out by the* TENANTS, *and accompanied to the door by* CLARA. *To the* TENANTS.) Thank you all very much indeed. I'm awfully sorry to have bothered you all.

A TENANT: Not at all, Signora Gala.

A TENANT: Don't mention it.

A WOMAN TENANT: After all, we're neighbours—and if neighbours don't help each other . . .

A TENANT: What scoundrels!

A WOMAN TENANT: We can't be safe even in our homes these days.

A TENANT: But perhaps, Signora Gala—seeing that they begged your pardon . . .

SILIA: Oh, no! They were told several times that this was a respectable place, and in spite of that . . . Really, you wouldn't believe the improper suggestions they dared to make to me.

A TENANT: Yes, you were quite right to take no excuses, Signora Gala.

A TENANT: Oh, you've done the right thing, there's no doubt about that.

A TENANT: They must be given a good lesson. You poor dear! Horsewhipping would be too good for them.

SILIA: I know the name of one of them. He gave me his card.

A TENANT: Who is he?

SILIA (showing the card): Marquis Aldo Miglioriti.

A WOMAN TENANT: Oh! Marquis Miglioriti!

A WOMAN TENANT: A Marquis!

ALL: He ought to be ashamed of himself! Disgraceful! A marquis to behave like that! That makes his behaviour all the worse! (etc.)

SILIA: You agree then that I had every right to be annoyed?

A WOMAN TENANT: Oh, yes! You're perfectly justified in teaching them a lesson, Signora Gala.

A WOMAN TENANT: They must be shown up, Signora. Shown up!

A TENANT: And punished!

A TENANT: They ought to be publicly disgraced!

A TENANT: But don't be too upset, Signora Gala.

A WOMAN TENANT: You ought to rest a little.

A WOMAN TENANT: Yes. It would do you good . . . after such an experience!

A WOMAN TENANT: Yes, we'll leave you now, dear.
ALL TENANTS: Good-night, Signora Gala ... (*etc.*) (*They leave.*)

As soon as the TENANTS *have gone,* SILIA *looks radiantly at* MIGLIORITI's *card, and laughs with gleeful, excited and malicious triumph. Meanwhile* GUIDO *is hammering on the door, right, with his fists.*

SILIA. All right! All right! All right! I'm coming! (SILIA *runs and unlocks the door.* GUIDO, *trembling with rage and indignation.*)
GUIDO: Why did you lock me in? I was longing to get my hands on them. My God, if I could only have got at those ruffians!
SILIA: Oh, yes, it only needed you to come dashing to my defence out of my bedroom to compromise me and ... (*with a mad glint in her eyes,*) ... spoil everything! (*showing him* MIGLIORITI's *card.*) Look. I've got it! I've got it!
GUIDO: What?
SILIA: One of their visiting cards!
GUIDO (*reading it—with surprise*): Marquis Miglioriti? I know him well. But what do you propose to do?
SILIA: I've got it, and I'm going to give it to my husband!
GUIDO: To Leone? (*He looks at her in terrified astonishment.*) But, Silia! (*He tries to take the card from her.*)
SILIA (*preventing him*): I want to see if I can't cause him (*Sarcastically*) just the 'slightest little bit of bother.'
GUIDO: But do you realise who this man is?
SILIA: Marquis Aldo Miglioriti.
GUIDO: Silia, listen to me! For goodness sake get this idea out of your head.
SILIA: I'll do nothing of the sort. **You** needn't worry. He'll realise that my lover couldn't possibly have come forward to defend me.
GUIDO: No, no, Silia, I tell you. You mustn't! I'll stop you at all costs!
SILIA: You'll stop nothing! In the first place, you can't ...

GUIDO: Yes I can, and will! You'll see!

SILIA: We'll see about that tomorrow. (*Imperiously*) I've had enough of this. I'm tired.

GUIDO (*in a threatening tone*): Very well. I'm going.

SILIA (*imperiously*): No! (*She pauses, then changes her tone.*) Come here, Guido!

GUIDO (*not altering his attitude, but going nearer to her*): What do you want?

SILIA: I want . . . I want you to stop being such a silly spoil-sport. (*Pause. She laughs to herself, remembering.*) Those poor boys! You know, I really did treat them rather badly.

GUIDO: As a matter of fact you did. After all, they admitted they'd made a mistake. And they begged your pardon.

SILIA (*curt and imperious again, admitting no discussion on the point*): That'll do, I tell you. I don't want to hear any more about that. I'm thinking of how funny they looked, poor boys. (*With a sigh of heart-felt envy.*) Such wonderful fantasies men get hold of at night! What fun they have! Moonlight, and . . . Do you know, Guido, they wanted to see me dance . . . in the square . . . (*Very softly, almost in his ear.*) Naked.

GUIDO: Silia!!!

SILIA (*leaning her head back and tickling his face with her hair.*) Guido . . . do you remember calling me a wayward child? (*Seductively*) I want to be your wayward child.

GUIDO (*embracing her*): Silia . . .

CURTAIN

ACT II

A room in LEONE GALA's *flat.*

It is an unusual room, fitted up to be at the same time a dining-room and a study. There is a dining table laid for lunch—

*and a writing desk covered with books, papers and writing materi-
al. There are glass-fronted cabinets filled with sumptuous silver
epergnes and cruets, a fine porcelain dinner service, and valuable
wine glasses—and bookshelves lined with solid-looking volumes.
In fact, all the furniture accentuates the dual function of the room,
with the exception of a third, occasional table on which there are
a vase of flowers, a cigar box and an ash tray.*

At the back, a door connects this room with LEONE's *bedroom. To the left, a door leads to the kitchen. To the right is the
main door into the room from the hall.*

Time: The next morning.

When the curtain rises, LEONE, *in cook's cap and apron is
busy beating an egg in a bowl with a wooden spoon.* PHILIP,
also dressed as a cook, is beating another. GUIDO VENANZI,
seated, is listening to LEONE.

LEONE: Yes, my dear Venanzi, he's so rude to me sometimes.
    You must wonder why I put up with him.

PHILIP (*surly and bored*): Don't talk so much—and carry on
    beating that egg.

LEONE: Do you hear that, Venanzi? Anyone would think he
    was the master and I the servant. But he amuses me. Philip
    is my 'tame devil.'

PHILIP: I wish the devil would fly away with you.

LEONE: Tt, tt . . . Now he's swearing. You see? I can hardly
    talk to him!

PHILIP: There's no need to talk. Keep quiet. (LEONE *laughs*.)

GUIDO: Really, Socrates!

PHILIP: Now, don't **you** start calling me Socrates. I've had
    enough of it from the master. To hell with Socrates. I don't
    even know who he is.

LEONE: What! (*Laughing*) You don't know him?

PHILIP: No, Signore! And I don't want to have anything to do
    with him. Keep an eye on that egg.

LEONE: All right! I'm watching it.

PHILIP: How are you beating it?

LEONE: With a spoon, of course.

PHILIP: Yes, yes! But which side of the spoon are you using?

LEONE: Oh, the back. Don't worry!

PHILIP: You'll poison that gentleman at lunch, I tell you, if you don't stop chattering.

GUIDO: No, no, Philip. Let him go on. I'm enjoying myself.

LEONE: I'm emptying him out of himself a bit, to give him an appetite.

PHILIP: But you're disturbing **me**.

LEONE (*laughing*): And 'me' is the only one who matters! Now we've come to the point!

PHILIP: You've hit it. What are you doing now?

LEONE: What am I doing?

PHILIP: Go on beating that egg, for goodness' sake! You mustn't slacken or you'll ruin it.

LEONE: All right, all right!

PHILIP: Have I got to keep my eyes on what he's doing, my ears on what he's saying, and my mind—that's already in a whirl—on all the tomfoolery that comes out of his mouth? I'm off to the kitchen!

LEONE: No, Philip—don't be a fool. Stay here. I'll be quiet. (*To* GUIDO, *sotto voce, but so that* PHILIP *can hear*.) He used not to be like this. Bergson has done for him.

PHILIP: Now he's trotting out that Bergson again!

LEONE: Yes, and why not? (To GUIDO.) D'you know, Venanzi, since I expounded to him Bergson's theory of intuition, he's become a different man. He used to be a powerful thinker . . .

PHILIP: I've never been a thinker, for your information! And if you go on like this, I'll drop everything here and leave you, once and for all. Then you'll really be in the soup!

LEONE (*to* GUIDO): You see? And I'm not allowed to say Bergson has ruined him! Mark you, I quite agree with what you say about his views on reason . . .

PHILIP: Well, if you agree there's nothing more to be said! Beat that egg!

LEONE: I'm beating it, I'm beating it! But listen a moment: according to Bergson, anything in reality that is fluid, living, mobile and indeterminate, lies beyond the scope of reason . . . (*To* GUIDO, *as though in parenthesis*,) though how it manages to escape reason, I don't know, seeing that Bergson is able to say it does. What makes him say so if it isn't his reason? And in that case, it seems to me it can't be **beyond** reason. What do you say?

PHILIP: Beat that egg! (*He is exasperated.*)

LEONE: I am beating it, can't you see? Listen Venanzi . . .

GUIDO: Oh, do stop calling me by surname; everyone calls me Guido.

LEONE (*with a strange smile*): I prefer to think of you as Venanzi. Anyway, listen: it's a fine game reason plays with Bergson, making him think she has been dethroned and slighted by him, to the infinite delight of all the feather-brained philosophising females in Paris! He maintains that reason can consider only the identical and constant aspects and characteristics of matter. She has geometrical and mechanical habits. Reality is a ceaseless flow of perpetual new-ness, which reason breaks down into so many static and homogeneous particles . . . (*During this speech,* LEONE, *as he gets worked up, gradually forgets his egg-beating, and finally stops.* PHILIP *always watching him and beating his own egg, approaches him stealthily.*)

PHILIP (*leaning forward and almost shouting at him*): And what are you doing now?

LEONE (*with a start, beginning to beat again*): Right you are! I'm beating the egg! Look!

PHILIP: You're not concentrating! All this talk about reason is taking your mind off what you're supposed to be doing.

LEONE: How impatient you are, my dear fellow! I'm perfectly well aware of the necessity of beating eggs. (*He beats rapid-ly.*) As you see, I accept and obey this necessity. But am I not allowed to use my mind for anything else?

GUIDO (*laughing*): You really are wonderful! The pair of you!

LEONE: No, no! You're wrong there! I'm wonderful if you like. But **he**, for a long time now—since he has been cor-rupted by Bergson, in fact . . .

PHILIP: No one has corrupted me, if you don't mind!

LEONE: Oh yes, my dear chap! You've become so deplorably human that I don't recognise you any more. (PHILIP *is about to remonstrate.*) Do let me finish what I'm saying, for

goodness' sake. We must have a little more emptiness to make
room for all this batter. Look! I've filled the bowl with my
energetic beating! (*There is a loud ring at the front door.*
PHILIP *puts down his bowl and goes towards the door on the
right.*)

LEONE (*putting down his bowl*): Wait. Wait. Come here. Untie
this apron for me first. (PHILIP *does so.*) And take this into
the kitchen too. (*He takes off his cap and gives it to* PHILIP.)

PHILIP: You've done it an honour, I must say! (*He goes off to
the left, leaving the apron and cap in the kitchen, and returns
a moment later, during the ensuing conversation between
LEONE and GUIDO, to collect the two bowls of batter and
take them into the kitchen. He forgets to answer the bell.
GUIDO gets up, very worried and perplexed at the sound of
the bell.*)

GUIDO: Did . . . did someone ring?

LEONE (*noting his perturbation*): Yes. Why? What's the matter?

GUIDO: Good God, Leone. It must be Silia.

LEONE: Silia? Here?

GUIDO: Yes. Listen, for heaven's sake. I came early like this,
to tell you . . . (*He hesitates.*)

LEONE: What?

GUIDO: About something that happened last night . . .

LEONE: To Silia?

GUIDO: Yes, but it's nothing, really. Just something rather
silly. That's why I haven't said anything to you. I hoped that
after sleeping on it she would have forgotten all about it.
(*Renewed, louder ringing at the door.*)

GUIDO: But there she is—that must be Silia!

LEONE (*calmly, turning towards the door on the left*): Socrates! For goodness' sake go and open the door!

GUIDO: Just a minute. (*To* PHILIP, *as he enters.*) Wait! (*To*
LEONE.) I warn you, Leone, that your wife intends to do
something really crazy . . .

LEONE: That's nothing new!

GUIDO: . . . at **your** expense. She wants to make you suffer
for it.

LEONE: Make me suffer, eh? (*To* PHILIP.) Let her in. Go and open the door! (*To* GUIDO.) My dear Venanzi, my wife is always sure of a welcome when she comes to visit me on that sort of business! (PHILIP, *more irritated than ever, goes to open the door*.)

GUIDO: But you don't know what it is!

LEONE: It doesn't matter what it is! Let her go ahead. You'll see! Remember what I do with the egg? I catch it, I pierce it, and I suck the yolk out of it.

GUIDO: Oh, damn your egg! (SILIA *enters like a whirlwind*.)

SILIA: Oh, so you're here, Guido! I suppose you came to warn him.

SILIA (*looking closely at* LEONE): I can see he knows.

LEONE: I don't know anything. (*Assuming a light, gay tone*.) Good morning!

SILIA (*quivering with rage*): Good morning, indeed! If you've told him Guido, I'll never . . .

LEONE: No, no, Silia. You can say what you've come to say without any fear of losing the effect of complete surprise you've been looking forward to. He's told me nothing. However, go out if you like, and make your entry again, in order to come upon me unexpectedly.

SILIA: Look here, Leone, I've not come here for fun! (*To* GUIDO.) What are you doing here, then?

GUIDO: Well, I came . . .

LEONE: Tell her the truth. He came to warn me, sure enough, of some crazy plan or other of yours.

SILIA (*exploding*): Crazy plan, you call it!

GUIDO: Yes, Silia.

LEONE: But he hasn't told me. I must admit I wasn't really interested to know.

GUIDO: I hoped you wouldn't come here . . .

LEONE: . . . so he didn't say a word about it, you see!

SILIA: How do you know it's 'one of my crazy plans', then?

LEONE: Oh, that I could imagine for myself. But, really . . .

GUIDO: I did tell him that much—that it was a crazy plan! And I stick to it!

SILIA (*exasperated to the utmost*): Will you keep quiet! No one

has given you the right to criticise the way I feel about things!
(*She pauses, then, turning to* LEONE, *as though shooting him
in the chest*.) You've been challenged!

LEONE: I've been challenged!

GUIDO: Impossible.

SILIA: Yes, you have.

LEONE: Who has challenged me?

GUIDO: It's impossible, I tell you.

SILIA: Well, I don't really know whether he's challenged you,
or whether you have to challenge him. I don't understand
these things. But I do know that I've got the wretched man's
card . . . (*She takes it out of her bag*.) Here it is. (*She gives it
to* LEONE.) You must get dressed at once, and go and find
two seconds.

LEONE: Hold on. Not so fast!

SILIA: No, you must do it now. Don't pay any attention to what
he says! He only wants to make you think this is 'one of my
crazy plans' because that would suit him.

LEONE: Oh, it would suit him, would it?

GUIDO (*furiously indignant*): What do you mean?

SILIA: Of course it suits you to put that idea into his head.
Otherwise you'd still be making the same excuses for that
. . . that scoundrel!

LEONE (*looking at the card*): Who is he?

GUIDO: Marquis Aldo Miglioriti.

LEONE: Do you know him?

GUIDO: Very well indeed. He's one of the best swordsmen in
town.

SILIA: Ah, so that's why!

GUIDO (*pale, quavering*): That's why what? What do you
mean?

SILIA (*as though to herself, scornfully, disdainfully*.) That's
why! That's why!

LEONE: Am I going to be allowed to know what's happened?
Why should I be challenged? Or why should I challenge
anybody?

SILIA (*in a rush*): Because I've been insulted, and outraged
and indecently assaulted—in my own home, too! And all

through you—because I was alone and defenceless! Grossly insulted! They put their hands on me, and mauled me about— (*touching her breast*,) here, do you understand? Because they thought I was . . . Oh! (*She covers her face with her hands and breaks out in harsh, convulsive sobs of shame and rage.*)

LEONE: But I don't understand. Did this Marquis . . .

SILIA: There were four of them. You saw them yourself as you were leaving the house.

LEONE: Oh, those four men who were by the front door?

SILIA: Yes. They came up and forced the door.

GUIDO: But they were tight. They didn't know what they were doing!

LEONE (*his voice heavy with mock astonishment*): Hello! Were you still there? (*The question puts* SILIA *and* GUIDO *at a loss. There is a pause.*)

GUIDO: Yes . . . but . . . I wasn't . . .

SILIA (*suddenly plucking up courage again, aggressively*): Why should he have protected me? Was it his job to do so when my husband had just that very moment turned his back, leaving me exposed to the attack of four ruffians, who, if Guido had come forward . . .

GUIDO (*interrupting*): I was in the . . . next room, you see, and . . .

SILIA: In the dining-room . . .

LEONE (*very calmly*): Having another liqueur?

SILIA (*in a furious outburst*): But do you know what they said to me? They said, 'If you've got a gentleman in there, carry on, don't mind us.' It only needed him to show himself, for me to be finally compromised! Thank goodness he had enough sense to realise that and keep out of sight!

LEONE: I understand, I understand! But I am surprised, Silia more than surprised—absolutely amazed to find that your pretty little head could ever have been capable of such clear discernment!

SILIA (*tonelessly, not understanding*): What discernment?

LEONE: Why, that it was up to **me** to protect you, because, after all, I am your husband, while Venanzi here . . . If he had attempted to stop those four drunks . . . By the way, he must have been more than a little drunk himself . . .

GUIDO: Nonsense! I tell you I didn't come in because I thought it more discreet not to!

LEONE: And you were quite right not to, my dear chap! What is so wonderful is that that pretty little head was able to understand that 'discretion' of yours, and could grasp that you would have compromised her if you had shown yourself. So she didn't call you to her aid, though she was being attacked by four dangerous drunks!

SILIA (*quickly, almost childishly*): They were crowding round me, all of them, clutching at me and trying to tear my clothes off . . .

LEONE (*to* GUIDO): And yet she actually managed to think matters out calmly and decide that this was something which concerned me! That is such a miracle that I am absolutely ready, here and now, to do without further delay, everything that can be expected of me!

GUIDO (*quickly*): What? You'll do it?

SILIA (*stupefied, turning pale, hardly believing her ears*): Do you mean that?

LEONE (*softly and calmly, smiling*): Of course I'll do it! Naturally! I'm sorry, but you're not logical!

GUIDO (*in a stupor*): Who? Me?

LEONE: Yes, you, you! Don't you see that my doing it is the exact and inevitable consequence of your 'discretion?'

SILIA (*triumphant*): You can't deny that's true!

GUIDO: How? (*Bewildered*) I don't understand. Why is it the consequence of my discretion?

LEONE (*gravely*): Just think a bit! If she was outraged like this, and you were quite right to act so discreetly, it obviously follows that I must be the one to issue the challenge!

GUIDO: Not at all. Not at all. Because my discretion was due to . . . because . . . because I realized that I should have had to deal with four men who were so drunk that they didn't know what they were doing!

SILIA: That's a lie!

GUIDO: Listen, Leone. They were drunk and they mistook the door. Anyway, they apologized.

SILIA: I didn't accept their apologies. It's easy to make excuses afterwards. I couldn't accept. But by the way Guido's talking anybody would think they had apologized to him! As though he was the one who'd been insulted! While all the time he kept himself well out of it, 'because he thought it would be more discreet!'

LEONE (*to* GUIDO): There! Now you're spoiling everything, my dear fellow.

SILIA: It was **me** they insulted. Me!

LEONE (*to* GUIDO): It was her. (*To* SILIA.) And you immediately thought of your husband, didn't you? (*To* GUIDO.) I'm sorry Venanzi. It's obvious you don't think things out properly.

GUIDO (*exasperated, noting* SILIA's *perfidy*): Why should I think things out? I kept out of it last night, and you can leave me out of it now!

LEONE (*conceding the point and continuing in the same solemn tone*): Yet you were right, you know, quite right to say that you would have compromised her. But not because they were drunk! That might, if anything, be an excuse for **me** . . . a reason why I should not challenge them, and call upon them to make amends for their behaviour . . .

SILIA (*dismayed*): What?

LEONE (*quickly*): I said 'if anything', don't worry! (*To* GUIDO.) But it can't possibly be an excuse for your discretion, because . . . well, if they were drunk you could perfectly well have been less 'discreet.'

SILIA: Of course he could! Men in their condition wouldn't have been shocked to find me entertaining a man in my flat. It wasn't yet midnight, after all!

GUIDO (*roused*): Good Lord, Silia. Now you have the impertinence to suggest I ought to have done what you prevented!

LEONE (*precipitately*): No, no, no, no! He acted quite rightly—you said so yourself, Silia. Just as **you** were right to think of me! After all, Venanzi, when a lady is being assaulted by drunks, her mental processes may be a little unpredictable.

No, you both acted perfectly correctly.

GUIDO: Look, just leave me out of it, will you? There isn't one consistent argument in the whole affair.

LEONE: That's where you're wrong, my dear friend. Silia's behaviour was perfectly consistent. After all, I am her husband—just as she is still my wife. And you . . . Why, of course, you are going to be 'The Second'.

GUIDO (*exploding*): Oh no, I'm not! You can get that idea out of your head!

LEONE: Why not, pray?

GUIDO: Because I flatly refuse!

LEONE: You do?

GUIDO: Yes.

LEONE: But you are bound to accept. You can't help yourself.

GUIDO: I tell you I won't do it.

SILIA (*bitingly*): Another sample of his 'discretion'.

GUIDO (*exasperated*): Silia!!!

LEONE (*conciliating*): Come now, please! Let us discuss the matter calmly. (*To* GUIDO.) Now, Venanzi, do you deny that everybody calls upon your services in affairs of honour? Not a month passes without your having a duel on your hands. Why, you're a professional second! Come now, it would be ridiculous. What would people say—those who know you're such a close friend of mine and so experienced in these matters—if I, of all people, should turn to someone else!

GUIDO: There's absolutely no occasion for a duel at all.

LEONE: That's not for you to say!

GUIDO: Well, I'm saying it. I'm not going to do it.

SILIA: I forced that man to leave me his card, and I showed it to everybody.

LEONE: Oh? The entertainment had an audience then?

SILIA: They heard me shouting for help. And they all said it would be a good thing to teach the Marquis a lesson.

LEONE (*to* GUIDO): There! You see! A public scandal! (*To* SILIA.) You're right! (*To* GUIDO.) Come, come. It's no use arguing, my dear chap. Besides, you have so much experience in these affairs. Everyone calls upon your services when they want a second. (GUIDO *gives up the position he has been maintaining, in the hope of getting on the right side of* SILIA *once more.*)

GUIDO: Oh, all right then! I'll cart you off to the slaughter, if you insist!

SILIA (*beginning to think better of it, since she finds herself left alone*): Oh, Guido! Don't exaggerate now!

GUIDO: To the slaughter, Silia! He will have it, so I shall take him off to the slaughter.

LEONE: No . . . Really, you know, my wishes don't come into it. You're the one who **will** have it.

SILIA: But it isn't necessary to fight a duel to the death.

GUIDO: That's where you are wrong, Silia. You either fight or you don't fight. If there is a duel, it has to be fought in deadly earnest.

LEONE: Of course, of course!

SILIA: Why?

GUIDO: Because the mere fact of my going to demand a meeting would show that we don't consider they were drunk.

LEONE: Quite right.

GUIDO: And the insult they did to you becomes doubly serious.

LEONE: Exactly.

SILIA: But it's up to you to suggest the terms—and you can make them easier.

GUIDO: How can I?

LEONE: Quite right. (*To* SILIA.) He can't.

GUIDO: Moreover, if Miglioriti finds we are making no allowance for the state he was in, or for his apology . . .

LEONE: Yes, yes!

GUIDO: . . . he'll be so angry . . .

LEONE: Naturally enough!

GUIDO: . . . that he'll insist on the severest possible terms!

LEONE: It will seem a great provocation to him—a swordsman!

GUIDO: One of our best swordsmen, as I told you. Consider that point very carefully! And you don't even know what a sword looks like!

LEONE: That's your worry. You don't expect me to concern myself with details like that, do you?

GUIDO: What do you mean, my worry?

LEONE: Because I'm certainly not going to worry about it.

GUIDO: You mean . . . It's my responsibility . . . to . . .

LEONE: It's all yours! And a very serious one. I feel sorry for you. But you must play your part, just as I am playing mine. It's all in the game. Even Silia has grasped that! Each of us must play his part through to the end. And you may rest assured that I shan't budge from my anchorage, come what may! I'm watching us all play our roles—and I find it vastly entertaining. (*The doorbell rings again.* PHILIP *enters from the left. He crosses the stage in a furious temper and goes out to the right.*) All that interests me is to get the whole thing over quickly. You go ahead and arrange everything . . . Oh, by the way, do you need any money?

GUIDO: Money? Good Lord, no! Why?

LEONE: I've been told these affairs are expensive.

GUIDO: Well, we'll go into that later. Not now.

LEONE: Very well, we'll settle up afterwards.

GUIDO: Will Barelli suit you as a witness?

LEONE: Oh, yes . . . Barelli . . . or anyone you please. (PHILIP *comes in again with* DR SPIGA.) Ah—Doctor Spiga. Come in, come in! (*To* GUIDO *who has approached* SILIA *and is pale and agitated.*) Look, Venanzi, we've even got the Doctor here. How convenient!

GUIDO: Good morning, Doctor.

LEONE: If you have confidence in him . . .

GUIDO: But really . . .

LEONE: He's a good chap, you know. First rate surgeon. But I don't want to put him to too much trouble, so I'm wondering—(*He turns to* GUIDO *who is talking to* SILIA.) I say, do listen! You've left us standing here like a couple of hermits in the wilderness! I was going to say, the orchard is conveniently near, we could do it there, early tomorrow morning.

GUIDO: Yes, all right, leave it to me, leave it to me! Don't interfere! (*He bows to* SILIA.) Good-bye, Doctor. (*To* LEONE.) I'll be back soon. No, wait, though! I shall have a lot to do. I'll send Barelli to you. I'll see you this evening. Good-bye. (*He goes out to the right.*)

SPIGA: What's all this about?

PHILIP: I say, don't you think it's about time . . .

LEONE: One moment, Socrates. Come over here, Spiga. First, let me introduce you to my wife . . .

SPIGA (*puzzled*): Oh, but . . .

LEONE (*to* SILIA): Doctor Spiga, my friend, fellow tenant, and intrepid opponent in philosophical arguments!

SPIGA: Charmed, Signora. (*To* LEONE.) So, you two have . . . ('*Made up*' *is understood.*) . . . *Well, I congratulate you; though, no doubt, to me it will mean the loss of a valued companionship to which I had become accustomed.*

LEONE: Oh, no! What are you thinking?

SPIGA: That you and your wife have . . .

LEONE: A reconciliation? But my dear fellow! We've never quarrelled. We live in perfect harmony—apart!

SPIGA: Oh . . . Well, in that case, I beg your pardon. I . . . I must confess I couldn't see what my being a surgeon had to do with a reconciliation. (PHILIP *comes forward, unable to contain any longer his furious indignation against his master.*)

PHILIP: It has a lot to do with it, Doctor. And your surgery is only one of the absurd, mad things that go on here!

LEONE: Really, Philip, I . . .

PHILIP: Oh, I'm off, I'm off! I'm leaving you right here and now! (*He goes to the kitchen, slamming the door.*)

LEONE: Spiga, go with him and try to calm him, will you? Bergson, my dear fellow, Bergson! Disastrous effect! As you said when I gave him the book, 'Once he starts studying logic and reason, there'll be no living with him.' (SPIGA *laughs, then, pushed by* LEONE *towards the door on the left, turns to bow to* SILIA, *then looks at* LEONE.)

SPIGA: But I still don't see how my surgery comes into it!

LEONE: Go on, go on! He'll explain it to you!

SPIGA: Hm! (*He leaves.* LEONE *goes to* SILIA *and stands behind the low chair in which she is sitting, absorbed. He leans over and looks down at her.*)

LEONE (*gently*): Well, Silia? Have you something else to say to me?

SILIA (*speaking with difficulty*): I never . . . never imagined . . .
   that you . . .
LEONE: That I?
SILIA: . . . would say 'yes'.
LEONE: You know very well that I have always said 'yes' to
   you. (SILIA *jumps to her feet, a prey to the most disordered
   feelings. Irritation with her husband's docility, remorse for
   what she has done, disdain for the shuffling perfidy of her
   lover. She is distracted to the point of weeping.*)
SILIA: I can't stand it! I can't stand it!
LEONE (*pretending not to understand*): What? My having said
   'yes?'
SILIA: Yes, that too! Everything . . . all this . . . (*Alluding to*
   GUIDO.) It will be your fault if it turns out to Guido's ad-
   vantage!
LEONE: My fault?
SILIA: Yes yours! Through your insufferable, limitless apathy!
LEONE: Do you mean apathy in general—or towards you?
SILIA: Your complete indifference, always! But especially
   now!
LEONE: You think he has taken advantage of it?
SILIA: Didn't you see him just now? Changing sides at every
   moment—but at the end, he still goes off to commit you to a
   duel.
LEONE: Aren't you being a little unfair to him?
SILIA: But I did tell him to try to make the terms easier, and
   not to go too far now . . .
LEONE: But at first you egged him on.
SILIA: Because he denied everything!
LEONE: That's true. He did. But, you see, he thought your
   attitude mistaken.
SILIA: And you? What do you think?
LEONE (*with a shrug*): I agreed to the duel.
SILIA: I suppose you think I exaggerated, too. Perhaps I did a
   little—but that was only because of the way he behaved.
LEONE: But wasn't that what you wanted?
SILIA (*distracted*): Yes . . . No . . . Oh, I can hardly remember
   now what it was I did want!

LEONE: You see, Silia, you always let emotion get the upper hand.

SILIA (*after a pause, looking at him in stupefaction*): And you? Still unmoved?

LEONE: You must allow me to protect myself as best I can.

SILIA: Do you really think this indifference of yours can help you?

LEONE: Certainly! I know it can.

SILIA: But he's an expert swordsman!

LEONE: Let Signor Guido Venanzi worry about that! What does it matter to me what this fellow is?

SILIA: You don't even know how to hold a sword!

LEONE: It would be useless to me. This indifference will be weapon enough for me, be sure of that! There I have an inexhaustible source of courage—not merely to face one man, that's nothing—but to face the whole world, always. I live in a realm where no anxieties can trouble me, my dear. I don't have to worry about anything—not even death—or life! Just look at the ridiculous absurdity of men and their miserable, petty opinions! Don't you worry! I understand the game. (*The voice of* PHILIP *is heard in the kitchen.*)

PHILIP: Well, go in your birthday suit, then! (SPIGA *comes in, left.*)

SPIGA (*as he enters*): In my birthday suit, indeed! Damned insolence! Oh ... I beg your pardon, Signora. Leone, that manservant of yours is an absolute demon.

LEONE (*laughing*): What's the matter?

SPIGA: What's all this I hear about a duel? Are you really involved in one?

LEONE: Do you find that difficult to believe?

SPIGA (*glancing at* SILIA, *embarrassed*): Well ... er ... no! To tell you the truth, I really don't know what the devil that fellow has been telling me. You've actually sent the challenge, have you?

LEONE: Yes.

SPIGA: Because you considered ...

LEONE: ... that I had to, of course. My wife has been insulted.

SPIGA (*to* SILIA): Oh, in that case—your pardon, Signora. I
   didn't realise. I . . . I . . . won't interfere. (*To* LEONE.) As a
   matter of fact, you know, I . . . I've never been present at a
   duel!
LEONE: Neither have I. So that makes two of us. It will be a
   new experience for you.
SPIGA: Yes, but . . . I mean . . . What about the formalities?
   How should I dress, for example?
LEONE (*laughing*): Oh, now I understand! That's what you
   were asking Socrates?
SPIGA: He told me to go naked. I shouldn't like to cut a poor
   figure.
LEONE: My poor friend, I'm afraid I can't tell you what doc-
   tors wear at duels. We'll ask Venanzi. He'll know.
SPIGA: And I must bring my surgical instruments, I suppose?
   (PHILIP *comes in from the left.*)
LEONE: Certainly you must.
SPIGA: It's on . . . serious terms, Philip tells me.
LEONE: So it seems.
SPIGA: Swords?
LEONE: I believe so.
SPIGA: If I bring my little bag . . . That'll be enough, eh?
LEONE: Listen—it's going to take place only a stone's throw
   away—in the orchard—so you can easily bring anything you
   feel you may need. (*The doorbell rings.* PHILIP *leaves to
   answer it.*)
SILIA: Surely that can't be Guido back so soon?
SPIGA: Venanzi? Oh, good. Then I can get him to tell me what
   I should wear. (PHILIP *comes in again and crosses the stage
   towards the door on the left.*)
LEONE: Who was it?
PHILIP (*loudly, drily and with an ill grace*): I don't know.
   Some man or other with a sword. (PHILIP *goes to the kitchen.*
   BARELLI *enters, right, with two swords in a green baize
   cover under his arm, and a case containing a pair of pistols.*)
BARELLI: Good morning.
LEONE (*going to meet* BARELLI): Come in, come in, Barelli.
   What's all this arsenal for?

BARELLI (*indignantly puffing*): Oh, I say, you know, look here, my dear Leone: this is absolute madness! Sheer raving lunacy! (*He sees* LEONE *pointing to* SILIA.) Eh? What? What's that?

LEONE: May I introduce you to my wife? (*To* SILIA.) This is Barelli—a formidable marksman!

BARELLI (*bowing*): Signora.

LEONE (*to* BARELLI): Doctor Spiga.

BARELLI: How do you do?

SPIGA: Delighted. (*He shakes* BARELLI's *hand, then, without releasing it, turns to* LEONE.) May I ask him?

LEONE: Not now. Later.

BARELLI: I've never heard of such a preposterous business in all my life. (*To* SILIA.) You must excuse me, Signora, but if I didn't say so I should be neglecting my plain duty. (*To* LEONE.) You don't mean to tell me you've actually sent an unconditional challenge?

LEONE: What does that mean?

BARELLI: What!!! You've issued one without even knowing what it is?

LEONE: How on earth should I know anything about such matters!

SILIA: Please—what is an unconditional challenge?

BARELLI: One that can't be discussed. It gives us no chance to try and settle the difference without fighting. It's against all the rules and quite illegal—prohibited under the severest penalties. And there are those two maniacs with the terms fixed up already—almost before they've set eyes on each other. By the way they were carrying on, it's a wonder they haven't decided on bombs and cannon as well.

SPIGA: Cannon?

SILIA: What do you mean?

BARELLI: Oh, the whole thing's crazy enough for that! First an exchange with pistols.

SILIA: Pistols?

LEONE (*to* SILIA): Perhaps he's arranged that to avoid swords, you know. I expect Miglioriti is not so clever with a pistol.

BARELLI: Who, Miglioriti? Why that fellow shoots the pip off the ace of spades at twenty paces!

SILIA: Was it Venanzi who suggested pistols?

BARELLI: Yes, Venanzi. What's the matter with him? Has he gone mad?

SILIA: Oh, my God!

SPIGA: But . . . excuse me, I don't follow. Where does the ace of spades come in?

BARELLI: What ace of spades?

LEONE: Quiet, quiet, Spiga. You and I don't understand these things.

BARELLI: First there's to be an exchange of two shots with pistols. Then you fall to with swords!

SILIA: Swords as well? Pistols weren't enough for him!

BARELLI: No, Signora—swords were chosen by agreement. Pistols were thrown in as an extra—out of bravado, as it were.

SILIA: But this is murder!

BARELLI: Yes, Signora. That's just what it is. But, if I may say so, it's up to you to stop it.

SILIA: Up to me? No! He's the one who can say the word! My husband. I never wanted it to become so serious.

LEONE: That's enough, Barelli. There's no point in starting a discussion with my wife now.

BARELLI: But, you don't understand! The whole town is full of this affair. They're talking about nothing else.

LEONE: Already.

SILIA: And I suppose they all say I am to blame.

BARELLI: No, no. Not you. Guido Venanzi, Signora. You understand, Leone, nothing is being said against you. You don't come into it at all, in fact. Miglioriti's furious against Guido since he found out that Guido was in the flat the whole time—hiding in the bedroom. (*To* LEONE, *with pained sympathy.*) Sorry, old boy! If he'd only come out and told Miglioriti it was all a mistake . . . After all, they were only drunk, you know . . . They'd have had a good laugh and there'd be no need for all this scandal. You need never have known, Leone . . . Or, at least you'd have been offered the chance to blink an eye. Instead of which, that damned fool lets the entire block of flats be called in to witness. And now he has the audacity to turn up at Miglioriti's as the bearer of a challenge!

SPIGA: Listen, Leone, perhaps—as a friend of both parties—I could do something . . .

LEONE (*in a sudden outburst*): Don't interfere, Spiga.

SPIGA: But, surely . . . since it is to take place so near here . . .

BARELLI: Yes, in the orchard—at seven tomorrow morning. Look, I have brought two swords.

LEONE (*quickly, pretending not to understand*): Have I to pay you for them?

BARELLI: Pay? Good Lord, no! They're mine. I want to give you a little elementary instruction, and let you get the feel of it.

LEONE (*calmly*): You want **me** to practise?

BARELLI: Of course! Who else? Me?

LEONE (*laughing*): No, no, no, no, thank you. It's quite unnecessary.

BARELLI: But I doubt if you've ever seen a sword, let alone handled one. (*He takes out one of the swords.*)

SILIA (*trembling at the sight of the sword*): Please! Please!

LEONE (*loudly*): That will do, Barelli! Let's have no more of these jokes.

BARELLI: Jokes?! You must at least learn how to hold the damn thing!

LEONE: That will do, I tell you. (*Firmly*) Listen, all of you, I don't want to appear rude, but I'd like to be left alone now.

BARELLI: Yes, of course, you must conserve your nervous energy. It's most important that you should keep calm.

LEONE: Oh, I shall keep calm, all right. When Guido comes back you two can amuse yourselves with those gadgets while I watch. Will that do? Meanwhile leave them here—and don't be annoyed if I ask you to go.

BARELLI: Only trying to help, old chap.

LEONE: You too, doctor, if you don't mind.

SPIGA: But won't you let me . . . ?

LEONE (*interrupting*): You'll be able to ask Barelli for all the information you want.

BARELLI (*bowing to* SILIA): Good-bye, Signora. Terribly sorry! (SILIA *barely inclines her head.*)

SPIGA: Good-bye, dear lady. (*He shakes her hand. To* LEONE.) Calm, you understand . . . calm . . . !

LEONE: Yes, all right. Good-bye.

BARELLI: Till this evening, then.

LEONE: Good-bye. (BARELLI *and* SPIGA *leave.*)

LEONE: Thank heaven they've gone.

SILIA: Do you . . .

LEONE: No, you stay if you like—provided you don't speak to me about this business.

SILIA: That wouldn't be possible. And then you'd never be sure of what I may do if Guido comes back, as he may at any moment. (LEONE *laughs loud and long.*)

SILIA: Don't laugh. Don't laugh!

LEONE: I'm laughing because I'm genuinely amused. You can't imagine how much I am enjoying watching you chop and change like this.

SILIA (*on the point of weeping*): But doesn't it seem natural to you?

LEONE: Yes, and that's just why I'm enjoying it: because you're so natural!

SILIA (*promptly, furiously*): But **you** are not!

LEONE: Isn't that a good thing?

SILIA: I don't understand you! I don't understand you! I don't understand you! (*She says this, first with almost wild anguish, then with wonder, then in an almost supplicating tone.*)

LEONE (*gently, approaching*): You can't, my dear! But it's better so, believe me. (*Pause. Then, in a low voice.*) I understand!

SILIA (*scarcely raising her eyes to look at him, terrified*): What do you understand?

LEONE (*calmly*): What it is you want.

SILIA: What do I want?

LEONE: You know—and yet you don't know what you want.

SILIA: I think I must be going mad!

LEONE: Mad? Oh, no!

SILIA: Yes. I must have been mad last night. I'm terrified.

LEONE: Don't be afraid! I'm here.

SILIA: What are you going to do?

LEONE: What I have always intended to do ever since you made me see the necessity.

SILIA: I?

LEONE: You.

SILIA: What necessity?

LEONE (*softly, after a pause*): To kill you! Do you think you haven't given me the motive to do it, more than once? Yes, of course you have! But it was a motive that sprang from a feeling—first of love, then of hate. I had to disarm those two feelings—to empty myself of them. And because I **have** emptied myself of them, now I can let the motive drop, and permit you to live. Not as you want to live— you don't know that yourself—but as you **can** live, and are bound to, seeing that it is impossible for you to do as I do.

SILIA: What do you do?

LEONE (*with a vague sad gesture, after a pause*): I set myself apart. (*Pause*) Do you imagine that impulses and feelings don't arise in me too? They do, indeed they do. But I don't let them loose. I cage them, like wild beasts at a fair. And I am their tamer. Yet I laugh at myself sometimes as I watch myself playing this self-imposed role of tamer of my feelings. At times, I confess, a desire comes upon me to let myself be mangled by one of those wild beasts—and, by you, looking at me now so meekly, so contritely. But that would be the last trick in the game: that would take away for ever the pleasure of all the rest.

SILIA (*hesitant, as though offering herself*): Do you want me to stay?

LEONE: Why?

SILIA: Or shall I come back tonight, when all the others have gone?

LEONE: No, no, thank you. I shall need all my strength.

SILIA: I mean, to be near you . . . To help you . . .

LEONE: I shall sleep . . . As I always do, without dreams.

SILIA (*with profound grief*): That's why everything's hopeless, you see! You won't believe it, but in bed my real love is sleep—sleep that quickly brings me dreams!

LEONE: Oh, yes, I believe you.

SILIA: But it never happens now. I can't sleep. And imagine what it will be like tonight! (*She breaks off.*) Well—I shall be here in the morning.

LEONE: Oh, no, no! You mustn't come. I don't want you to.

SILIA: You're joking!

LEONE: I forbid you to come.

SILIA: You can't stop me.

LEONE: Very well. Do as you please. (*At this point* PHILIP *enters, left—with the lunch tray.*)

PHILIP (*in a hollow, surly, imperious voice*): Hey! Lunch is ready!

SILIA: Till tomorrow morning, then. (*She gazes at* LEONE *with deep longing. If he were only to give a sign, she'd be prepared to become his again forever. But he is as impassive as ever.*)

LEONE (*submissively*): Till tomorrow morning . . .

SILIA *goes out.* LEONE *closes the door behind her and stands for a moment, lost in thought. Then he moves slowly towards the table and seats himself at the end of it, absently unrolling his napkin.*

CURTAIN

ACT III

LEONE's *flat early the next morning. When the curtain rises, the stage is empty and almost dark. The front door bell rings.* PHILIP *enters left, and crosses the stage.*

PHILIP: Who the devil's calling on us at this hour? What a day! (*He goes out, right. After a moment he enters with* DR SPIGA, *who is dressed in frock coat and top hat, and carries two large bags full of surgical instruments.*)

SPIGA: Good morning, Philip.

PHILIP: 'morning, Doctor.

SPIGA (*surprised at not seeing* LEONE): How is he?

PHILIP: He's still asleep, so don't talk so loudly.

SPIGA: Good God, he's still asleep and I haven't shut my eyes all night!

PHILIP: What have you got there? (*He points to the two bags.*)

SPIGA: All my instruments—everything! (*He goes to the dining table which* PHILIP *has already partly laid.*) Now . . . Take off this tablecloth.

PHILIP: What for?

SPIGA: I brought my own. (*He takes a surgical sheet of white American cloth out of one of the bags.*)

PHILIP: What are you going to do with that?

SPIGA: I'm going to get everything laid out in readiness here.

PHILIP: Oh, no, you're not! You're not touching this table. I'm just laying it for breakfast.

SPIGA: Breakfast? Lord, man! This is no time to be thinking about breakfast!

PHILIP: You leave this table alone!

SPIGA (*turning to the writing desk*): Well, clear the desk then.

PHILIP: Are you joking? If the police find out about the duel, don't you know that these two tables can talk?

SPIGA (*testily*): Oh, yes! I know all about that. Don't you start quoting **him** at me! I've heard it before! Two symbols: writing desk and dining table; books and cooking utensils; the void and the counter balance! I know, I know. But haven't you realized that in half an hour from now all those nonsensical ideas of his may be snuffed out like a candle?

PHILIP: I suppose you've ordered his coffin, too! You look like an undertaker.

SPIGA (*exasperated*): My God, what an unfeeling brute you are! They told me to dress like this. This is really the limit. Heaven alone knows what a night I've had . . .

PHILIP: Not so loud! You'll wake him up!

SPIGA (*softly*): . . . I haven't time to argue with you. Clear this other little table for me then. (*He points to the third, smaller one.*) And get a move on.

PHILIP: Oh, I don't mind your using **that** one. It won't take long. (*He removes a cigar-box and a vase of flowers.*) There you are—cleared.

SPIGA: At last. (SPIGA *spreads his cloth on the table and begins to get out his instruments. At the same time* PHILIP *goes on laying the breakfast table, occasionally disappearing into the kitchen to fetch things. The conversation continues meantime.*)

SPIGA (*to himself, checking his instruments*): Scalpels ... bone saw ... forceps ... dissectors ... compressors ...

PHILIP: What do you want all the butcher's shop for?

SPIGA: What do I want it for! Don't you realize he's going to fight a duel? Suppose he gets shot in a leg or an arm? We may have to amputate.

PHILIP: Oh, I see. Why haven't you brought a wooden leg, then?

SPIGA: You never know what may happen with firearms; you have to be prepared for anything. Look, I've brought these other little gadgets for bullet extraction. Probe ... mirror ... electric torch ... scissors ... two types of extractor ... Look at this one! English model—a beauty isn't it? Now, where did I put the needles? Let ... me ... see ... Hm ... (*He looks in one of the bags.*) Ah, here they are! I think that's everything. (*Looks at the clock.*) I say, it's twenty-five past six! The seconds will be here any minute!

PHILIP: So what? It's got nothing to do with me!

SPIGA: I was thinking of him—suppose he isn't awake yet!

PHILIP: It's too early for him.

SPIGA: It's no good trying to keep him to his timetable today! He made the appointment for seven o'clock.

PHILIP: Then he'll have to wake himself up.

SPIGA: Perhaps he's up already. You might go and see!

PHILIP: Look ... I'm his clock on ordinary days and I know the hours I've got to keep ... and I'm not putting myself a minute fast or slow, today or any other day. Reveille, seven thirty ...

SPIGA: Good God man! Don't you realise that at seven-thirty today he may be dead?

PHILIP: . . . and at eight I bring him his breakfast! (*There is a ring at the front door bell.*)

SPIGA: There! You see? That'll be the seconds. (PHILIP *goes out. He comes back shortly after with* GUIDO *and* BAREL-LI.)

GUIDO (*as he enters*): Ah, good morning, Doctor.

BARELLI (*ditto*): Good morning, Doctor.

SPIGA: Good morning. Good morning.

GUIDO: Are we all ready?

SPIGA: I am, quite ready!

BARELLI (*laughing at the sight of all the surgical armoury laid out on the table*): He certainly has got everything ready!

GUIDO (*irritated*): Well, good God there's nothing to laugh at!

BARELLI (*with amused curiosity as he picks up an instrument*): What on earth's this? (SPIGA *sharply takes away the object.*)

SPIGA (*rather crossly*): Well, it **was** sterilized. (*He replaces it, but away from the others.*)

GUIDO (*with a shudder*): Terrifying collection! Has **he** seen it?

SPIGA: Who? Excuse me . . . *Quod abundat non vitiat.*

GUIDO: I'm asking you whether Leone has seen these instruments. (*To* BARELLI.) You know, he must be absolutely calm, but if he sees . . .

SPIGA: Oh, no, he hasn't seen anything yet!

GUIDO: Where is he?

SPIGA: Well . . . I think he's not up yet.

BARELLI: What?

GUIDO: Not up yet?

SPIGA: I **think**, I said. I don't **know**. He hasn't been in here.

GUIDO: Well, we can't stand about here like this. We have only a quarter of an hour left. He must be up. (*To* PHILIP.) Go and tell him we are here.

BARELLI: What a man!

GUIDO (*to* PHILIP, *who has remained motionless, frowning*): Get a move on!

PHILIP: At seven-thirty!

GUIDO: Oh, go to blazes! I'll call him myself. (*He rushes to the door at the back.*)

SPIGA: He's bound to be up.

BARELLI: He really is amazing, upon my word!

GUIDO (*knocking loudly on the door, centre, and listens with his ear to it*): What can he be doing? Surely he isn't still asleep? (*He knocks again, louder and calls.*) Leone! Leone! (*He listens.*) He is still asleep! My God, he's still asleep! (*He knocks again and tries to open the door.*) Leone? Leone!

BARELLI: He really is amazing, you know—quite amazing!

GUIDO: How does he lock himself in?

PHILIP: With the bolt.

GUIDO: But why?

PHILIP: I don't know.

BARELLI: Does he always sleep as soundly as this?

PHILIP: Like a log! Two minutes, it takes me to wake him, every morning.

GUIDO: Well, I'll wake him if I have to smash the door in! Leone! Leone! Ah, he's awake at last! (*Speaking through the door.*) Get dressed quickly. Hurry up. Hurry up. It's almost seven already.

BARELLI: Would you believe it!

SPIGA: What a sound sleeper!

PHILIP: Yes, he's always the same. He has to drag himself out of his sleep as if he was hauling himself up from the bottom of a well!

GUIDO: Oh, is there any danger of his falling back again? (*He turns back to look at* LEONE's *door.*)

BARELLI (*hearing a noise*): No, listen. He's opening the door.

SPIGA (*placing himself in front of the table with his instruments*): I'll keep him away from here! (LEONE *appears, perfectly placid and still rather sleepy, in pyjamas and slippers.*)

LEONE: Good morning.

GUIDO: Go and get dressed at once. You haven't a minute to lose.

LEONE: Why, may I ask?

GUIDO: He asks why!

BARELLI: Have you forgotten you've a duel to fight?

LEONE: I? Fight a duel?

SPIGA: He's still asleep!

GUIDO: The duel, man! The duel! At seven o'clock.

BARELLI: In less than ten minutes.

LEONE: Don't get excited, I heard.

GUIDO (*absolutely dumbfounded*): Well then?

LEONE: Well then what?

BARELLI (*also dumbfounded*): What do you mean 'what'?! You've got to get dressed and go and fight!

LEONE (*placidly*): Have I?

SPIGA (*as though to himself*): He must have gone out of his mind!

LEONE: No, Doctor! I'm perfectly *Compos mentis*.

GUIDO: You have to fight.

LEONE: I have to fight, too, have I?

BARELLI: 'Too'? What do you mean?

LEONE: Oh, no, my friends. You're mistaken!

GUIDO: Do you want to withdraw?

BARELLI: Don't you want to fight, now?

LEONE: I? Withdraw? But you know perfectly well that I always firmly maintain my position.

GUIDO: I find you like this, and yet . . .

BARELLI: But, if you say . . .

LEONE: How do you find me? What do I say? I say that you and my wife upset my whole day yesterday, Venanzi, trying to make me do what I admitted all the time was my duty.

GUIDO: But . . . but . . ,

BARELLI: You're going to fight!

LEONE: That's not my duty.

BARELLI: Whose is it, then?

LEONE (*pointing to* GUIDO): His!

BARELLI: Guido's?

LEONE: Yes, his. (*He goes to* GUIDO, *who has turned pale.*) And you know it. (*To* BARELLI.) He knows it! I, the husband, issued the challenge, because he couldn't for my wife's sake. But as for fighting the duel, oh no! As for fighting the duel . . . (*To* GUIDO *softly, pulling one of the lapels of his jacket, and stressing every word,*) . . . you know quite well, don't you, that that is no concern of mine, because I never fight against anybody. You're the one who fights! (GUIDO, *in a cold sweat, passes a hand across his brow.*)

BARELLI: This is fantastic!

LEONE: No, Barelli, perfectly normal, I assure you! Quite in accordance with the rules of the game. I'm playing my part: he's playing his. I am not going to budge from my anchorage. And his opponent looks at it as I do. You said yourself, Barelli, that the Marquis is really angry with him, not with me. Because they all know, and you better than any of them, what he wanted to do to me. Yes, Venanzi, you and Silia really did want to cart me off to the slaughter, didn't you?

GUIDO (*protesting vigorously*): No, **I** didn't! **I** didn't!

LEONE: Oh, yes, yesterday, you and my wife were like two children bouncing up and down on a see-saw. And I was in the middle, balancing myself and you two into the bargain.

GUIDO: Leone, I assure you . . .

LEONE: You thought you'd have a little game with me, didn't you? You thought between you, you could win my life from me? Well, you've lost the game, my friends. I have outplayed you.

GUIDO: No! You are my witness that yesterday, right from the beginning, I tried . . .

LEONE: Oh yes, you **tried** to be discreet. Very discreet!

GUIDO: What do you mean? What are you insinuating?

LEONE: You must admit, my dear fellow, that you didn't carry your discretion quite far enough—did you? At a certain point—for reasons which I understand quite well; indeed, I feel quite sorry for you—at a certain point your discretion failed you. And now, I regret to say, you are about to suffer the consequences.

GUIDO: Because you're not going to fight?

LEONE: Exactly. It's not my business.

GUIDO: Very well, then. Is it mine?

BARELLI (*rising*): 'Very well', do you say?!

GUIDO (*to* Barelli): Wait! (*To* LEONE.) What are you going to do?

LEONE: I'm going to have breakfast.

BARELLI: But this is fantastic!

GUIDO: No, I mean . . . Don't you realise that if I take your place . . .

LEONE: No, no, my dear Venanzi! Not mine. Your own!

GUIDO: Very well, if I take **my** place, don't you realize that **you** will be dishonoured!

BARELLI: Disgraced! We shall be forced to expose your dishonour! (LEONE *laughs loudly*.)

BARELLI: How can you laugh? You'll be dishonoured, dishonoured!

LEONE: I understand, my friends, and I can still laugh. Don't you see how and where I live? Why should I worry my head about honour?

GUIDO: Don't let's waste any more time. Let's go.

BARELLI: But are you really going to fight this duel?

GUIDO: Yes, I am. Don't you understand?

BARELLI: No, I don't!

LEONE: Yes, it really is his business, you know, Barelli!

BARELLI: You're being cynical!

LEONE: No, Barelli, I'm being rational! When one has emptied oneself of every passion and . . .

GUIDO (*interrupting and gripping* BARELLI *by the arm*): Come, Barelli. It's no use arguing now. And you too Doctor— you'd better come with us.

SPIGA: I'm coming! I'm coming! (*At this moment*, SILIA *enters, right. There is a short silence, during which she stands still, perplexed and amazed.* GUIDO *comes forward, very pale, and grasps her hand.*)

GUIDO: Good-bye, Silia. (*He turns to* LEONE.) Good-bye. (GUIDO *rushes out, right, followed by* BARELLI *and* SPIGA.)

SILIA: Why did he say good-bye like that?

LEONE: I told you, dear, that it was quite useless for you to come here. But you were determined to.

SILIA: But . . . What are you doing here?

LEONE: Don't you know? I live here!

SILIA: And what is Guido doing? Isn't . . . Isn't the duel going to take place?

LEONE: Oh, it will take place, I suppose. It may be taking place now!

SILIA: But . . . How can it be? If you're still here?

LEONE: Oh, yes, I am here. But he has gone. Didn't you see him?

SILIA: But then . . . That means . . . Oh, God! Why has he gone? Has he gone to fight for you?

LEONE: Not for me—for you!

SILIA: For me? Oh, God! Did you do this? (LEONE *comes close to her, with the commanding, disdainful air of a cruel judge.*)

LEONE: Did I do this? You have the impertinence to suggest that I am responsible?

SILIA: But you have . . .

LEONE (*in a low voice, gripping her arm*): I have punished you both!

SILIA (*as though biting him*): I see! But at the price of your own dishonour!

LEONE: You are my dishonour.

SILIA: And all this time . . . God, what can be happening to him? It's horrible. Is he down there fighting? Fighting on **those** terms!

LEONE (*quickly*): Upon which he himself insisted. (SILIA *suddenly laughs hysterically.*)

SILIA: Oh, it's perfect, perfect! And you let him have his way. I swear he never intended to fight, not he! You are the devil! The devil incarnate! Where are they fighting? Tell me! Down there? In the orchard? (*She looks for a window.*)

LEONE: It's no good, you know. There aren't any windows over-looking the orchard. You must either go down or climb up onto the roof.

At this point, DR SPIGA, *pale and dishevelled in grotesque discomposure, dashes in; flings himself at his surgical instruments laid out on the table, rolls them up in the cloth, and rushes out without saying a word.*

SILIA: Doctor! Tell me . . . Tell me . . . What's happened? (*Not believing her own presentiments.*) Dead? (*Running out after him.*) Tell me! Is he dead? Tell me?

LEONE *remains motionless, absorbed in deep, serious thought. A long pause.* PHILIP *enters, left, with the breakfast tray and puts it down on the table.*

PHILIP (*calling in a hollow voice*): Hey! (LEONE *barely turns his head.* PHILIP *indicates the breakfast with a vague gesture.*) Breakfast time!

LEONE, *as though he has not heard, does not move.*

CURTAIN

EACH IN HIS OWN WAY

Ciascuno a suo modo

1924

Translated by
Felicity Firth

CHARACTERS

'Fixed' characters who appear on the 'stage':

DELIA MORELLO
MICHELE ROCCA
DONNA LIVIA PALEGARI, an elderly lady
HER GUESTS
DORO PALEGARI, her son
DIEGO CINCI, his young friend
FILIPPO, manservant to the Palegari household
FRANCESCO SAVIO, who opposes Doro
PRESTINO, his friend
SAVIO'S FENCING-COACH
HIS MANSERVANT

'Fluid' characters who appear in the theatre foyer and passages:

LA MORENO (well-known to all)
BARON NUTI
THE ARTISTIC DIRECTOR
ACTORS AND ACTRESSES
THE THEATRE MANAGER
THE COMPANY'S ADMINISTRATIVE DIRECTOR
THEATRE STAFF
POLICEMEN
FIVE DRAMA CRITICS
UNSUCCESSFUL OLD AUTHOR
YOUNG AUTHOR
LITERARY MAN (who doesn't write)
PLACID SPECTATOR
IRRITATED SPECTATOR
FAVOURABLE MEMBERS OF THE AUDIENCE (a few)
HOSTILE MEMBERS OF THE AUDIENCE (a good number)
SOCIALITE SPECTATOR
OTHER LADIES AND GENTLEMEN OF THE AUDIENCE

FOREWORD

A performance of this play should really begin outside on the street or better still in the forecourt of the theatre, with news-vendors shouting out headlines and distributing a specially printed news-sheet headed 'Late Night Extra'. The reason for the special edition is the unexpected leak to the press of the news item splashed in bold headlines across the front page in true journalistic manner:

SUICIDE OF SCULPTOR LA VELA
THE SUBJECT OF TONIGHT'S PLAY
AT . . . . . THEATRE
(Here give name of theatre.)

A sensational scandal is about to burst on the theatre world. Rumour has it that the subject of Pirandello's latest play, *Each in His Own Way*, due to be premiered tonight at the . . . . . Theatre, is the highly dramatic suicide of Giacomo La Vela, the deeply mourned young sculptor who took his own life some months ago in Turin. Readers will remember that La Vela came back one day to his studio to find his fiancée, the well-known actress A.M., in a compromising situation with Baron Nuti. Instead of attacking the guilty couple La Vela turned his weapon upon himself with fatal results.

It further appears that Baron Nuti was engaged to marry La Vela's sister. The shocking effect of the tragedy is still keenly felt by a wide circle of people, partly because of the professional recognition already achieved by the young sculptor, and partly because of the social prominence and indeed notoriety of the other two participants in the tragedy. It is more than likely that tonight's performance will result in some unpleasant repercussions.

Besides this, people queueing at the box office for tickets will catch sight of Amelia Moreno in the foyer (she is the A.M. referred to in the newspaper item) accompanied by three gentlemen in evening-dress, all vainly doing their utmost to dissuade her from coming to see the play. They urge her to be sensible, to come with them and at least keep out of the public view. It's not the place for her, they say, will she please let them take her home, surely she does not want to create a scandal? She is strained and tense and very pale, but refuses to co-operate. She is determined to stay and see the play; she wants to see just how far the author has dared to go. She gnaws nervously at a lace handkerchief. She lets herself be recognised and then does not know whether to hide or be angry. She keeps saying she wants a box in the third tier. She promises not to let herself be seen if her friends will go and buy the tickets. She undertakes not to create a scandal. She will leave if it gets too much for her. A box in the third row. Will they get it or shall she?

The above extemporised scene must be made as convincing as possible and should start a few minutes before the curtain is due to go up. It should continue until the bells ring for the performance to start and should provoke surprise, curiosity, and possibly even apprehension among members of the audience as they arrive at the theatre.

While this is going on, those spectators who have got as far as the corridor just outside the auditorium will experience even more surprise, curiosity, and possibly apprehension on finding a second scene taking place, this time between Baron Nuti and his friends.

'Don't worry! Don't worry! I'm perfectly calm! Just look how calm I am! I shall be even more calm, if you'll just leave me. It's you who are attracting attention, with your fuss! Leave me alone, and nobody will even look at me! I'm a member of the audience for heaven's sake! One among many! What else does one come to a theatre for! ... I know she will come ... perhaps she is here already. I just want to see her again, just see her. Yes, yes, yes, from a distance! That's all I want! Don't worry! Now for heaven's sake, will you go? Don't let me make a spectacle of myself in front of all these people—they have come to laugh at me behind my back! Look! I want to be left alone! How can I make myself clear? I'm calm, yes! Calm! I am utterly, totally calm!'

He continues to pace up and down, with stricken face and trembling body, until the audience has all gone into the theatre.

The above will serve to explain why the Management have seen fit to append a postscript to their notices advertising tonight's performance:

N.B. We are unable to state with any certainty whether the play tonight will consist of two acts or three. It is possible that circumstances beyond our control may prevent the performance from being completed.

ACT 1

The ancient family house of the aristocratic Donna Livia Palegari. She has been entertaining and her guests are about to leave. Through a triple archway on two columns at the back of the stage can be seen her luxurious and brilliantly lighted drawing-room, where a large number of guests still linger. The main stage is taken up with a smaller darker salon, an altogether sombre little room, its walls hung with damask and valuable paintings, largely on religious themes. The general impression is of a side-chapel in some great basilica, a sacred chapel in a profane temple, of which the vast reception-room beyond the archway might be said to constitute the nave. The only furniture in the smaller room is the odd bench or stool for the use of people who want to look at the pictures. There is no door. Guests wander in in twos and threes in search of a quiet spot to talk. When the curtain rises the room is occupied by an OLD FAMILY FRIEND and a SUBTLE YOUTH, whom we come upon in mid-conversation.

THE SUBTLE YOUTH (*a small, sore-looking head on his shoulders, like that of a plucked chicken*): What's your opinion then?

THE OLD FAMILY FRIEND (*handsome, authoritative, faintly malicious; with a sigh*): My opinion! (*A pause*) No idea! (*A pause*) What do other people say?

SUBTLE YOUTH: Well, some say one thing, some say another.

OLD FAMILY FRIEND: Of course they do. Everyone's entitled to a point of view.

SUBTLE YOUTH: But they don't seem all that sure about what they do think. Or, perhaps they just aren't saying until they've found out what everybody else thinks.

OLD FAMILY FRIEND: Well, I know perfectly well what I
 think. But one likes to be a bit cautious; one doesn't want to
 make irresponsible guesses; it's as well to know for instance,
 if others are party to some special information which might
 modify one's view.
SUBTLE YOUTH: All right, well, what's your opinion of the
 situation as far as you know it?
OLD FAMILY FRIEND: Dear boy, there will always be unknown factors!
SUBTLE YOUTH: Why bother to have opinions at all, then?
OLD FAMILY FRIEND: Well, good heavens, I mean, I know
 what I think—until somebody comes up with proof to the
 contrary!
SUBTLE YOUTH: But if I may say so, saying that there are
 always unknown factors is the same as saying that there is
 always proof to the contrary.
OLD FAMILY FRIEND: (*looks at him reflectively, then smiles
 and asks*): So this is your way of proving I have no opinion?
SUBTLE YOUTH: Well, according to what you have just said,
 it's impossible for anyone ever to have an opinion.
OLD FAMILY FRIEND: And isn't that in itself an opinion?
SUBTLE YOUTH: Ye-es, a pretty negative one!
OLD FAMILY FRIEND: Better than nothing! Better than nothing dear boy! (*He takes the young man's arm and returns with
 him to the large drawing-room at the back of the stage. There
 is a pause. Through the arches we see young girls still hand-
 ing round tea and cakes.* TWO YOUNG WOMEN *enter,
 clearly anxious not to draw attention to themselves.*
FIRST YOUNG WOMAN (*very keyed up and anxious*): Come
 on then, tell me, I can't wait! It's life or death to me to know
 about this!
SECOND YOUNG WOMAN: It was only an impression I had,
 just a sort of hunch!
FIRST YOUNG WOMAN: Even an impression means something. Was he looking pale? Did he have a sad sort of smile?
SECOND YOUNG WOMAN: I think perhaps he did.
FIRST YOUNG WOMAN: I shouldn't have let him go. I knew
 it really. I held onto his hand as far as the door. As he started

to walk away I was still holding it. We had kissed good-bye but our hands refused to let go. As soon as I got back in I just collapsed. I simply howled. I was completely shattered. But go on, tell me—did he say anything?

SECOND YOUNG WOMAN: What about?

FIRST YOUNG WOMAN: What I mean is, you know, even in general conversation, sometimes . . .

SECOND YOUNG WOMAN: He didn't speak. He just stood, really, listening to everybody else.

FIRST YOUNG WOMAN: That's because he knows. He knows how much people hurt each other . . . talking all the time. He knows that unless you're a hundred per cent certain of what you're saying, it's best to say nothing at all. Once you let yourself speak you can't really be sure what it is you are saying . . . Was he sad? Did he have a sad sort of smile on his face? Can you remember at all what the others were talking about?

SECOND YOUNG WOMAN: I honestly don't remember. And I really wouldn't want to raise false hopes. You know? . . . it's so easy to be mistaken. Perhaps he was just neutral and I only thought he was smiling a bit sadly. But, oh yes, wait! Somebody said . . .

FIRST YOUNG WOMAN: . . . what?

SECOND YOUNG WOMAN: Now what was it . . . yes . . . 'Women are like dreams, they are never quite what you'd like them to be.'

FIRST YOUNG WOMAN: **He** didn't say that, did he?

SECOND YOUNG WOMAN: Oh no.

FIRST YOUNG WOMAN: Oh God, I don't know! You see, now I start wondering whether I'm not making the most terrible mistake! I've always been on top of situations, done things my way! With him I'm always nice, but perhaps I should try being nasty! It might shake him!

SECOND YOUNG WOMAN: Oh, darling! Don't change! I'd hate you not to be yourself!

FIRST YOUNG WOMAN: But what is myself? I don't think I know! I'm sure I don't know! I keep shifting and changing and drifting. I twist and turn all over the place. One minute I laugh; the next minute I'm sobbing in a corner. It's a night-marish feeling! It's a horrible way to be! I keep running away from myself; I can't bear to look at myself; it's so shaming to keep changing all the time! *(Another group of guests ar-rives at this point: two very elegant rather blasé young men accompanied by* DIEGO CINCI)

FIRST YOUNG MAN: Shall we be in your way?

SECOND YOUNG WOMAN: Of course not. Please come in.

SECOND YOUNG MAN: Aha! The holy of holies! The con-fessional!

DIEGO: Confessions daily at six! Donna Livia should instal a priest and a grille for the convenience of her guests!

FIRST YOUNG MAN: Now confession is something I don't hold with! One has a conscience! What's wrong with good old conscience?

DIEGO: Good question! How do you use it, though?

FIRST YOUNG MAN: How do you use conscience?

SECOND YOUNG MAN (*solemnly*): *Mea mihi conscientia pluris est quam hominum sermo.*

SECOND YOUNG WOMAN: Good Lord! Is that Latin?

SECOND YOUNG MAN: Cicero, no less. I remember it from school.

FIRST YOUNG WOMAN: What does it mean?

SECOND YOUNG MAN: It means, 'For me what counts is my conscience, whatever the world may say.'

FIRST YOUNG MAN: It's quite straightforward. It's what we all say 'If your conscience is clear nothing else matters.'

DIEGO: You'd have to live on a desert island . . .

SECOND YOUNG MAN (*puzzled*): What do you mean?

DIEGO: . . . for that to be true. And in total isolation, you wouldn't even need your conscience. Unfortunately, my friends, we are not isolated. Here am I . . . and here are you. It's too bad!

FIRST YOUNG WOMAN: Why too bad?

SECOND YOUNG WOMAN: You're not very complimentary!

DIEGO: Because, ladies, we have to take account of others, always!

SECOND YOUNG MAN: I don't agree! **My** conscience is per-fectly adequate!

DIEGO: But what is conscience? It is the voice of others inside
   you!

FIRST YOUNG MAN: Sounds a bit paradoxical to me!

DIEGO: No, it isn't. (*To the* SECOND YOUNG MAN) When
   you talk about conscience being your guide, what exactly are
   you saying? You mean, don't you, that other people may think
   what they like about you, they may even misjudge you, but
   as long as you know you have done nothing wrong, your
   mind is easy. Is that right?

SECOND YOUNG MAN: That's right.

DIEGO: Well, that's fine. But who in the end is responsible
   for the fact that your mind is easy? It's other people, isn't
   it?

SECOND YOUNG MAN: No, it is not. It is me! My conscience! For heaven's sake!

DIEGO: No. It's because you think that anybody else in your
   place, given your circumstances, would have done the same
   thing! That's what it comes down to, old chap! Oh yes, I grant
   you, beyond one's immediate individual circumstances, well,
   obviously, there are certain general abstract principles which
   we can fairly easily agree over. But, do you see: when you
   shut yourself off in your high-handed way and insist that all
   you need is the voice of your own conscience, it's because
   you are aware of people's condemnation and disapproval and
   ridicule—otherwise you'd have no need to say it. The fact is
   that principles aren't much help; they are abstractions. Nobody else is going to apply them to your case, or bother to
   imagine what it feels like to be you. So where does your
   conscience actually get you? Does it help you, out there on
   a limb? Anything but. The loneliness is the most terrifying
   part. So what do you do? You conjure up a row of heads
   inside your head, each one an exact replica of your own; you
   put your case to them and pull a string and hey, presto! there
   they are, nodding and shaking, yes and no, yes when you
   want yes, no when you want no. You are reassured and con-
   firmed in your decision. So, right you are, carry on! It's a
   splendid sport! Hours of fun with the self-sufficient conscience!

FIRST YOUNG WOMAN: Look at the time! I must go!

SECOND YOUNG WOMAN: Goodness, yes. Look, everyone's going. (*To* DIEGO, *pretending to be shocked*.) You're disgraceful!

FIRST YOUNG MAN: Come on, it's time we were going too. (*They return to the larger room to thank their hostess and take their leave. The last guests are saying good-bye. When they have gone,* DONNA LIVIA *moves downstage, in a state of great agitation. She has asked* DIEGO CINCI *to remain behind. The* OLD FAMILY FRIEND *whom we saw at the beginning is with her, also a* SECOND OLD FRIEND.)

DONNA LIVIA (*to* DIEGO): Oh, my dear, don't go! You are Doro's closest friend. I'm at my wits' end! Tell me about my wretched son! Tell me this news isn't true!

OLD FAMILY FRIEND: It's only a rumour, Donna Livia; it may be quite unfounded!

DIEGO: What have they been saying? What's up with Doro?

DONNA LIVIA (*surprised*): Don't you know?

DIEGO: No, I don't. It can't be serious or I'd know.

SECOND OLD FRIEND (*half-closing his eyes as if to soften the blow*): Yesterday's scandal . . .

DONNA LIVIA: At the Avanzis' . . . Doro publicly defending that . . . what's her name? . . . that ghastly woman!

DIEGO: Was there a scandal? What ghastly woman?

OLD FAMILY FRIEND: The Morello woman . . . who else?

DIEGO: Ah. So it's about Delia Morello.

DONNA LIVIA: Do you know her, then?

DIEGO: My dear lady, who doesn't know her?

DONNA LIVIA: So Doro knows her? My God, it's all true! Doro knows her!

DIEGO: All right, so Doro knows her! Where's the scandal?

DONNA LIVIA (*to* OLD FAMILY FRIEND): And you said he didn't!

DIEGO: He only knows her in the way we all know her! What's it all about?

OLD FAMILY FRIEND: Look, I did say he probably hadn't met her to speak to . . .

SECOND OLD FRIEND: I expect he just knew **of** her . . .

DONNA LIVIA: But he was publicly defending her behaviour? . . . Ready to fight, you said . . .

DIEGO: Who was he going to fight with?

SECOND OLD FRIEND: . . . with Francesco Savio . . .

DONNA LIVIA: It's unbelievable! To take the thing so far! What
must the Avanzis have thought! And for a woman like that!

DIEGO: Well, you know what arguments are like . . .

OLD FAMILY FRIEND: . . . in a heated discussion . . .

SECOND OLD FRIEND: . . . it happens so easily . . .

DONNA LIVIA: Please, please! Don't try and cover up! (*To*
DIEGO) Diego, dear, come on, you tell me! You know Doro
best . . .

DIEGO: You mustn't worry, Donna Livia!

DONNA LIVIA: Now look! If you really are my son's friend,
it's your duty to tell me honestly what you know!

DIEGO: But I don't know anything at all! It will turn out to be
nothing! Just a few words . . . you can't let words upset you!

OLD FAMILY FRIEND: But that's not quite it . . .

SECOND OLD FRIEND: It certainly caused a stir, one can't
say it didn't . . .

DIEGO: But what, for heaven's sake?

DONNA LIVIA: His defending her like that! It was a scanda-
lous thing to do, you must see that!

DIEGO: Have you perhaps not realised, Donna Livia, that
people have been talking about Delia Morello now non-stop
for three weeks?. The subject has been chewed to death in
just about every corner of this city, in every café and drawing-room and newspaper office. You must have read something about her in the newspapers yourself.

DONNA LIVIA: I read that a man killed himself because of
her.

OLD FAMILY FRIEND: . . . a young painter: Salvi . . .

DIEGO: Giorgio Salvi, that's right.

SECOND OLD FRIEND: An exceptionally talented young
man, by all accounts . . .

DIEGO: . . . and it appears he wasn't the first.

DONNA LIVIA: What? Do you mean there have been others?

OLD FAMILY FRIEND: Yes, it was in some newspaper . . .

SECOND OLD FRIEND: What, another actual suicide?

DIEGO: A Russian chap, some years back, in Capri.

DONNA LIVIA (*beside herself with horror, her face in her hands*): Oh God, oh God!

DIEGO: Now don't you go worrying that Doro's going to be number three! The tragic death of a young artist like Giorgio Salvi is bound to inspire a lot of public sympathy; but it's not impossible that, once you know the full circumstances, there are things to be said on her side as well!

DONNA LIVIA: Are you on her side too?

DIEGO: Yes, I think so . . . I don't see why not!

SECOND OLD FRIEND: You would go right against public opinion?

DIEGO: Yes, I would! I could make out a case for her!

DONNA LIVIA: My Doro! For heaven's sake, he was always such a serious boy!

OLD FAMILY FRIEND: Reserved sort of chap . . .

SECOND OLD FRIEND: . . . dignified . . . !

DIEGO: He probably just went a bit too far, found himself cornered, and said more than he meant to.

DONNA LIVIA: Don't say any more! Just don't say any more! Is she an actress, this Delia Morello?

DIEGO: She's as mad as they come whatever she is!

OLD FAMILY FRIEND: She has been an actress, certainly.

DIEGO: She has got herself chucked out of all the theatre companies; they just can't take her eccentricity. They won't sign her up any more. 'Delia Morello' must be a stage name. God knows what her real name is, who she is and where she comes from!

DONNA LIVIA: Is she pretty?

DIEGO: Extremely pretty.

DONNA LIVIA: Wouldn't you know it! They always are! I suppose Doro met her at the theatre.

DIEGO: He may have seen her a time or two in her dressing-room; no more than that. But please don't worry! She's not nearly as alarming as people imagine!

DONNA LIVIA: Is she not? She's simply notched up a couple of suicides.

DIEGO: She wouldn't have driven me to suicide.

DONNA LIVIA: She drove two people out of their minds!

DIEGO: Well, she wouldn't drive me out of mine!

DONNA LIVIA: It's not you I'm afraid for! It's Doro!

DIEGO: Don't be afraid! Do realise that whatever harm the poor wretched girl may have done to others, she has done far worse to herself. She is a haphazard kind of creature, half-crazy most of the time, never knows where she is going or what she wants from life. Mostly she just looks like a frightened little girl asking for help.

DONNA LIVIA (*disturbed by this, clutching at* DIEGO's *arm*): I'll bet that's Doro you are quoting!

DIEGO: I am not quoting Doro.

DONNA LIVIA (*insisting*): Be honest with me, Diego, he's in love with her, isn't he?

DIEGO: I keep telling you: no, he's not!

DONNA LIVIA: Oh yes, he is! I know he is! You only say that kind of thing when you're in love!

DIEGO: But Doro never said it! I said it!

DONNA LIVIA: Nonsense, Diego! Of course Doro said it. Nothing you can say will convince me otherwise.

DIEGO (*momentarily cornered*): Oh God! (*With a change of tone, clear, cheerful, suddenly full of fun.*) Look! I know what you're thinking! In your mind's eye there's a carriage bowling along a country road—in open country on a lovely sunny day . . .

DONNA LIVIA (*puzzled*): A carriage? What on earth are you talking about?

DIEGO (*with another switch of mood, bitterly, moved by real feeling*): Do you know what happened to me the night my mother died? I was watching at her bedside and directly in my view there was an insect swimming in a glass of water. It had six legs, flat wings, and had fallen into a glass on the bedside table. And I never noticed the moment of my mother's death because I was so totally absorbed in the optimism of that tiny creature. He put so much faith in his hind legs. They were longer than the others, for hopping about I suppose. It was a desperate swim. He had got this fixed idea

that those two back legs were going to get him out of there;
any minute now he'd be catapulted to safety if he could just
kick away whatever it was that was clinging to his heels.
After each attempt to leap free he would clean the hind legs
with the front ones and then try again. I watched, fascinated,
for over half an hour. I watched him die . . . and missed
seeing my mother die. Do you see what I'm trying to say?
Perhaps now you can let me be.

DONNA LIVIA (*embarrassed, puzzled, exchanging a quick
glance with her two friends, equally embarrassed and puzzled*): I'm sorry, but I don't see the connection . . .

DIEGO: No, well, I daresay it seems absurd. But tomorrow
you'll see the funny side of it . . . really you will . . . you will
see the ridiculousness of being so worried over Doro if someone can some along and take your mind right off it with a red
herring like my carriage on a country road . . . Not quite such
a joke for me though, to think of the insect who diverted my
attention so that I missed my mother's dying breath. (*There
is a pause. After this unexpected digression* DONNA LIVIA
*and her two old friends exchange further glances. They are
profoundly baffled by their failure to see any connection
whatsoever between their previous conversation and*
DIEGO's *references to the carriage and the insect.* DIEGO
CINCI *meanwhile is genuinely distressed at the revived memory of his mother's death; so that* DORO PALEGARI, *who
comes in now, finds* DIEGO *not at all his usual self.*)

DORO (*looking round at all four, disconcerted*): Whatever's
the matter?

DONNA LIVIA (*recovering herself*): Ah, There you are, Doro!
Doro, dearest boy, what have you been up to? I've been
hearing all sorts of things . . .

DORO (*turning on her fiercely*): The scandal's reached you,
has it? You've heard that I'm in love with Delia Morello, is
that it? You've heard that I'm besotted, obsessed, insane with
love? I can tell you I got the full treatment this morning,
friends winking at me left and right as I came along: 'So it's
Delia Morello, is it?' Good God, what a world!

DONNA LIVIA: But Doro, you asked for it . . .

DORO: Asked for it? Christ, it's unbelievable! The thing's blown up into a scandal already!

DONNA LIVIA: ... taking her part like that ...

DORO: I took nobody's part!

DONNA LIVIA: ... at the Avanzis' last night ...

DORO: Last night at the Avanzis' I was present when Francesco Savio expressed an opinion I couldn't agree with. It was about a matter of common knowledge, the tragic death of Giorgio Salvi. I simply told him he had got his facts wrong.

DONNA LIVIA: But the things you said ...

DORO: Yes, I probably said some crazy things. I have no idea what I said. Once I get going I'll say anything. But one is entitled, is one not, to view the things that happen, each in his own way? It seems to me you can look at a thing in whatever way you like! You can see it like this today and like that tomorrow. I am perfectly prepared, if I see Francesco Savio tomorrow, to tell him he was right and I was wrong!

OLD FAMILY FRIEND: Well, that's all right then!

DONNA LIVIA: Well, Doro, dear, that's exactly what you must do!

SECOND OLD FRIEND: It would stop the tongues wagging!

DORO: I wouldn't do it to stop the tongues wagging. Let them wag! I'd do it because now I'm so angry with myself ...

OLD FAMILY FRIEND: Of course, dear boy, of course!

SECOND OLD FRIEND: Dreadful to be so sorely misunderstood!

DORO: It's not that. I am angry at having overstated my case. Francesco Savio was being fiendishly obstinate and totally illogical, but substantially he was quite right. Looking at it now in the cold light of day I'm prepared to admit he was right. I'll find a way of saying so in public and then perhaps this storm in a teacup might just die down. I've had enough of it!

DONNA LIVIA: Oh good! Oh, what a relief, Doro darling! It's splendid to hear from your own lips, in front of Diego, that you find the woman's behaviour indefensible!

DORO: Do you mean Diego was defending her too?

OLD FAMILY FRIEND: Well, yes, he said something like that ... he sort of said ...

SECOND OLD FRIEND: ... an academic point ... he was
  trying to pacify your mother.
DONNA LIVIA: Hardly the way to pacify me! Luckily my
  mind is now at rest, Doro, and I thank you for it.
DORO (*stung by the implications of this*): You can't be serious!
  God give me patience!
DONNA LIVIA: What's wrong with thanking you?
DORO: Well, for Christ's sake what are you thanking me for?
  I can only suppose you thought the rumours were true!
DONNA LIVIA: No, no! Of course I didn't
DORO: Then why do you thank me? Why do you say your mind
  is at rest 'now'? I shall go clean off my head in a minute!
DONNA LIVIA: I'm sorry, Doro, just forget I said it!
DORO (*turning to* DIEGO): What grounds do you defend her
  on, then, Diego? Delia Morello, I mean.
DIEGO: Can't we drop the subject? Now that your mother is
  reassured.
DORO: No, really, I'd like to know! I'd like to know!
DIEGO: So that you can reopen the debate with me?
DONNA LIVIA: Enough's enough, Doro dear!
DORO (*to his mother*): No, really, I'm curious ... (*to* DIEGO)
  ... to see how your arguments match up with the ones I used
  against Francesco.
DIEGO: And what if they do? Will you change sides again?
DORO: I'm not quite such a chameleon. My line of argument
  was this: Delia Morello cannot be said to have been plotting
  the ruin of Giorgio Salvi when she ran off with another chap
  the night before the wedding; because the real ruin of Giorgio
  Salvi anyway would have been marriage with Delia Morello!
DIEGO: Ah, right! Well, there you've got it! ... You know what
  a lighted torch in the sun looks like? You see them in funeral
  processions. You don't see the flame! All you see is smoke!
DORO: What are you trying to say?
DIEGO: Oh, that I agree! Delia Morello knew perfectly well
  what marriage would do to him—and that was the reason she
  didn't want it! But this doesn't show, you see, perhaps she
  can't even see it herself; all that anybody sees is the smoke,
  the apparent so-called betrayal.

DORO: I can't let you get away with that! She betrayed him all right! There's no question about that! And how exquisitely she did so! I've been thinking about it all day. She chose Michele Rocca to run off with as the supreme means of getting back at Salvi—exactly as Francesco Savio was saying yesterday.

DIEGO: Well, I suggest you stick with Savio's version, then, and let the whole subject drop.

OLD FAMILY FRIEND: Absolutely right! Best thing you could do! We'll be off then Donna Livia . . . (*He kisses her hand.*)

SECOND OLD FRIEND: . . . so glad it is all sorted out! (*He too, kisses her hand and then turns to the two young men.*) Good-night then, boys!

OLD FAMILY FRIEND: Good-bye, Doro. Good-night, Cinci.

DIEGO: Good-night. (*He draws him on one side and says softly, with a touch of malice.*) I congratulate you.

OLD FAMILY FRIEND (*astonished*): Whatever on?

DIEGO: On your capacity to hold something back. It's admirable. There's always that little something that does not quite come out.

OLD FAMILY FRIEND: I don't think I do, do I? What do you mean?

DIEGO: You must admit, you keep your thoughts very much to yourself, and you don't even let it show. We are very much alike, you and I!

OLD FAMILY FRIEND: H'm! I don't get it! What am I supposed to say!

DIEGO (*drawing him even further away from the others*): I wouldn't mind marrying her myself! But there we are, I have only just enough for one to live on. It would be like two people sharing one umbrella and both of them getting wet!

DONNA LIVIA (*who, satisfied that all is well, has been chatting with* DORO *and the* SECOND OLD FRIEND, *turning now to the* OLD FAMILY FRIEND, *who is laughing*): Well, old friend . . . and what's the joke?

OLD FAMILY FRIEND: Nothing at all. Just Diego's usual nonsense.

DONNA LIVIA (*taking his arm and guiding both* OLD
FRIENDS *out through the drawing-room to exit right*): . . .
and my dear, if you go to Christina's tomorrow tell her to be
ready on time! (DORO *and* DIEGO *are left alone. Behind
them the drawing-room, still ablaze with lights, looks odd
now that it is empty. There is a pause.*)

DIEGO (*holding up his hands for* DORO *to see, the fingers
intertwined in a kind of cat's cradle*): It's like this! This is
exactly how it is, look!

DORO: What?

DIEGO: Conscience, consciousness . . . what I was saying just
now. An elastic net. If you let it slacken, just a fraction, out
pops madness.

DORO (*perturbed and suspicious, after a pause*): Are you
referring to me?

DIEGO (*as if to himself*): Let the net slacken, and out it all
comes, all the flotsam of the mind, the disconnected images
of years, fragments of past life shoved out of sight because
they don't bear rational scrutiny; dubious actions, embarrass-
ing lies, resentment, ill-feeling, detailed private fantasies of
uncommitted crimes, inadmissible desires: out it pours, the
whole damn lot, appalling and horrifying.

DORO (*still worried*): What are you getting at?

DIEGO (*staring into space*): I had gone without sleep for nine
whole nights . . . (*He breaks off, turning suddenly to* DORO.)
You try it some time, nine nights without sleep! . . . there was
a little china cup on the bedside table, with a single blue band
round the rim. And then there was that infernal clock chiming
every blessed hour! Eight, nine, ten . . . I kept count . . .
eleven, twelve . . . not to mention the quarters. No human
affection can survive a test like that, the deprivation of the
body's basic need for sleep. I raged against the cruel fate that
was keeping my mother's body alive, and it was **just** her body
now, you see, insensible, just about unrecognisable, as I list-
ened to her breathing the deep raucous wheezing of the dying.
And do you know what I was thinking? I was thinking, 'Shut
up! For God's sake stop that ghastly breathing!'

DORO: But I thought your mother died two years ago, at least!

DIEGO: She did. Let me tell you what I caught myself doing. There was a moment when the breathing stopped. The silence was awful. I had leaned over her body to look close, to see if she were dead. And for some reason I turned my head towards the mirror in the wardrobe. My face looked back at me from the mirror, forcing me to take in my own expression as I hovered over my mother, scanning her face. It was an expression of jubilant astonishment and relief. Then she started breathing again. I was sickened by myself at that moment; I hid my face; I felt caught out in a crime. And then I started to cry. I was Mummy's little boy; I actually wanted her to take pity on me for being so tired. I was falling apart with tiredness. I didn't want her to be dead, now. I wanted my Mummy . . . the poor Mummy who always gave up sleep for me when I wanted her in the night.

DORO: But why bring this up now all of a sudden?

DIEGO: I've no idea. What about you? Do you know why you felt annoyed when your mother thanked you for reassuring her?

DORO: Well, like everybody else she was leaping to conclusions . . .

DIEGO: Oh yes? Come off it, Doro! You can't fool me!

DORO (shrugging): I don't know what you mean.

DIEGO: If it hadn't been true, you would just have laughed. You wouldn't have got annoyed.

DORO: Good Lord! **You** don't think, surely . . . ?

DIEGO: What am I supposed to think? It's you . . .

DORO: But I'm agreeing with Savio, now!

DIEGO: That's what I mean. You've done a complete turn-about. And you are cross with yourself for having over-stated the case for the defence.

DORO: Well, yes, because I've got it right now . . .

DIEGO: No! Be honest! Can you really not see what's in your mind?

DORO: Perhaps you would like to tell me!

DIEGO: You now reckon Savio's right. Do you know why? To stop yourself acknowledging a feeling inside you that you don't want to face.

DORO: That's rubbish! That's ridiculous!

DIEGO: It's a fact!

DORO: Ridiculous!

DIEGO: In the heat of discussion last night the feeling sur-
faced. It went to your head and made you say more than you
realised. I mean it! You don't know what goes on inside your
head. There are thoughts in there you aren't aware of!

DORO: What, for instance? And when did I think them?

DIEGO: You thought them without even knowing it. My dear
old boy, illegitimate thoughts are every bit as real as illegitimate children.

DORO: Yours may be!

DIEGO: Well, indeed yes, mine too! One's relationship with
one's mind is a kind of marriage. The mind we espouse is
chosen for its suitability—a partner who will help us realise
our aims and aspirations—and the arrangement lasts a lifetime. But outside the honest confines of wedlock, outside the
framework of the conscious mind, we get up to all sorts of
extra-marital adventures and lapses with the psyches we have
rejected, the partners we have turned away and relegated to
the basements of our being, and from these liaisons are born
actions and thoughts which we prefer not to acknowledge. If
forced to acknowledge them, then we may adopt them or
legitimise them, but with provisos and conditions and safe-
guards. I mean here are you, rejecting this poor little found-
ling thought of yours! Take a good look at it, though! There's
no doubt it's yours! You are in love with Delia Morello!
Madly, ridiculously in love!

DORO (*laughing*): You make me laugh . . . you make me laugh.
(*The butler*, FILIPPO, *enters from the drawing-room.*)

FILIPPO: Mr Francesco Savio is here.

DORO: Ah! Show him in, will you? (FILIPPO *withdraws.*)

DIEGO: I'll be off.

DORO: No, don't go. I want to show you whether or not I'm
in love with Delia Morello! (*Enter* FRANCESCO SAVIO.)
Come in, come in, Francesco.

FRANCESCO: Doro, old chap! Good evening, Cinci!

DIEGO: Good evening.

FRANCESCO (*to* DORO): I came to apologise for yesterday evening's quarrel.

DORO: Dear chap! I was planning to come and see you with exactly the same thing in mind!

FRANCESCO (*grasping him*): Well! What a relief! Well, well!

DIEGO: You make a very touching picture, the pair of you!

FRANCESCO (*to* DIEGO): Do you realise we were on the point of ruining a life-long friendship?

DORO: It wasn't as bad as that!

FRANCESCO: I think it was! I lay awake all last night kicking myself for not having seen his point of view, the generous point of view . . .

DIEGO (*quickly*): You call it generous now, do you? His defence of Delia Morello?

FRANCESCO: It was a courageous thing to do in front of that bloodthirsty mob . . .

DIEGO: You were one of the bloodthirstiest.

FRANCESCO (*warmly*): I was! I hadn't stopped to think! I hadn't properly considered Doro's arguments. When I did, I was utterly convinced.

DORO (*angry now*): Really? So now you think . . .

DIEGO: Ha! You're for the defence now, are you?

FRANCESCO: He risked his reputation! He stood his ground magnificently. He annihilated that bunch of ignoramuses with his answers and all they could do was snigger.

DORO (*exploding*): Francesco, you are an idiot! A prize idiot!

FRANCESCO: But I have come to tell you that you were right!

DORO: That's what I mean! That's why you're an idiot!

DIEGO (*to* FRANCESCO): He was on his way to tell you **you** were right!

FRANCESCO: To tell me I was right?

DIEGO: Yes, you. He saw the justice of your accusations against Delia Morello.

DORO: And now he has the gall to come round here and tell me I was right!

FRANCESCO: Because I've thought it over. I've thought out what you said.

DIEGO: That's right! And **he** has thought out what **you** said!

FRANCESCO: And now he thinks I was right?

DIEGO: And you think he was right.

DORO: Well, that's marvellous! You subject me to the mockery of that rabble; you expose me to the full battery of their spite; you cause considerable anxiety to my mother—

FRANCESCO: You're blaming me for all this?

DORO: I certainly am. You provoked me, you compromised me, you made me say all sorts of things I'd never have said without your provocation! (*He thrusts his face in* FRANCE-SCO's. *He is quivering with anger.*) So don't you dare go around saying that you now agree with me!

DIEGO (*driving home the message*): . . . and that you've come round to the generous point of view . . .

FRANCESCO: But I have!

DORO: You are an idiot!

DIEGO: People will just think you've changed your mind because now you know that Doro loves Delia, and that's why he stood up for her!

DORO: Lay off, Diego, for heaven's sake! I'm losing my temper fast! (*To* FRANCESCO) Idiot! Idiot! Idiot!

FRANCESCO: That's five times you've called me an idiot.

DORO: Oh, I can improve on that. I don't suppose I shall ever call you anything else.

FRANCESCO: I am in fact a guest in your house.

DORO: I don't care where you are. It won't stop me calling you an idiot.

FRANCESCO: Well, if that's how it is, OK I'll be off. (*Exit*)

DIEGO (*about to run after him*): Come back, Francesco! Don't be like that!

DORO (*restraining* DIEGO): Let him go!

DIEGO: You can't be serious. He means trouble.

DORO: I couldn't give a damn!

DIEGO (*breaking free of* DORO): This is stupid. I'm going after him. (*Exit*)

DORO (*calling after him*): Don't you dare interfere in my affairs. (DIEGO *does not return, and* DORO *starts pacing up and down muttering between his teeth.*) What the hell's he playing at! He has the nerve to come and tell me I was right, at this stage! Idiot! After mouthing off in front of all those people . . . (*Enter* FILIPPO, *looking faintly baffled, with a visiting card.*)

FILIPPO: Excuse me, sir.

DORO (*breaking off his monologue, brusquely*): What is it?

FILIPPO: A lady asking for you, sir.

DORO: A lady?

FILIPPO: Her card, sir. (*He hands it to him.*)

DORO (*profoundly shaken by the name he reads on the card*): You mean this lady is here? Where is she?

FILIPPO: She's waiting in the hall, sir.

DORO (*he stares about him, nonplussed; then attempts to hide his anxiety and agitation as he asks*): Has . . . er . . . my mother gone out?

FILIPPO: She went out a while ago, sir.

DORO: Show her in. Show her in. (*He goes into the large drawing-room to receive her. FILIPPO goes out and comes in with DELIA MORELLO. He brings her as far as the archway. She is soberly but very elegantly dressed, and wears a veil. FILIPPO bows and withdraws*).

DORO: Delia! What on earth are you doing here?

DELIA: I have come to thank you! Give me your hands! (*She grasps his hands.*)

DORO: No! Look here, you mustn't . . .

DELIA: Oh, yes! (*She tries to kiss his hands which she is still holding.*) Oh, yes! Oh, yes!

DORO: Wait a minute! Don't do that! It's I who should . . .

DELIA: I have come to thank you for what you have done!

DORO: I haven't done anything! All I did . . .

DELIA: Oh, that! Your great public defence! I didn't mean that! Whether people attack me or defend me hardly makes any difference! I am quite capable of tearing **myself** to pieces. No, I am thanking you for what you thought, what you felt, not for anything you shouted in public.

DORO (*uncertain how to react to this*): Well, all I thought was . . . well . . . knowing the facts, knowing what I knew . . . it just seemed . . . well, the right thing.

DELIA: Right or wrong, what does it matter! What matters is

that when I heard what you had said, I recognised myself. Do you understand? It was me! I recognised myself at once, in what you said about me.

DORO (*still embarrassed, but anxious not to show it*): I see . . . because . . . because I got it right then?

DELIA: So right! You got it so right you might have been me; except that you understood me in a way that I have never, never understood myself! When I heard it, it sent shivers up my spine! I shrieked 'Yes! That's it! That's right! That's absolutely right!' You can have no idea of what I felt, of how elated and how shaken I felt, realising, knowing in my bones, that that was me, that those motives you had uncovered were mine!

DORO: I'm glad, really glad! That's . . . that's good! I'm glad . . . because you see it came to me in a kind of flash. It just dawned on me; I didn't think it out. It was a kind of inspired glimpse into your mind. I suddenly saw it, and then later, I must admit, it went . . .

DELIA: It went?

DORO: But never mind! I mean, you say it was you! You recognised yourself!

DELIA: Doro, my dear. I have been living on your inspired glimpse ever since this morning. Of course that's what it was! So much so that I'm baffled as to how you could have arrived at it. I mean, you hardly **know** me, really know me. I struggle to know myself in a perfectly agonising way, but . . . I don't know . . . it's as if I were not inside myself! As if I were constantly chasing after the person I really am, trying to catch up with her and ask her what it is she wants, why she is unhappy, what can I do to calm her down and give her peace!

DORO: Ah, peace, yes! You could certainly do with some of that.

DELIA: I see him, you know, all the time. I see him the moment he collapsed in front of me . . . one minute his face was blazing down into mine and next it was drained white, and his body was slumped at my feet; I leant over to look at him and I felt sort of annihilated, destroyed by what I saw in his face in that dizzy moment: that suddenly he was dead for all eternity. In one split second I saw all memory, all thought wiped off his face forever. And I was the only one, the only one who knew what life had been in that poor shattered head blown to pieces because of a useless nobody like me! I was out of my mind. Imagine what I feel like now!

DORO: Do try to be calm!

DELIA: I can be calm, all right. I get so calm I seize up completely. It's like a kind of paralysis. My whole body goes numb. It really does. I clutch hold of myself and I can't feel anything. I look at my hands and it's as if they were somebody else's. And as for the things I'm supposed to do, well, for heaven's sake, I just don't see the point in doing them any more. I get the mirror out of my handbag and then what happens? Can you imagine, in this horrible blank frozen state, what it does to me to look in that little disc of mirror and see my painted mouth, my painted eyes? I don't have a face any more! I've traded it in for a mask!

DORO (*with feeling*): That's only because you can't see it as other people see it!

DELIA: There you go! Why is it, that whenever I think I have found somebody who at last will be able to help me sort myself out, I end up hating them! All they see is the eyes! And the mouth! They don't take a blind bit of interest in what really matters to me.

DORO: You mean the real 'you'.

DELIA: And so I punish them. Right there in the department they are most interested in. I find their excitement loathsome so to start with I work on it to tease them. The revenge is all the sweeter. Then I swoop; I throw this old body at the first bit of riff-raff. (DORO *nods knowingly, as if to say 'all too true'*.) . . . Just to show them! To show them how I despise the thing they value most in me (DORO *still nods*.) Am I my own worst enemy? Well, of course. I have always done myself more harm than good. But there, the great thing about poor riff-raff is at least they know they are poor riff-raff. They may be depressing but they don't disappoint you. They can even have a good side. It's quite a refreshing surprise sometimes to discover how undevious they can be!

DORO (*surprised*): This is what I said! Exactly what I said!

DELIA (*in tears*): . . . Well, that's how it was . . .

DORO: I told them! I told them you were unpredictable . . .

DELIA: . . . that I was given to mad fits . . . that's right! . . .
sudden aberrations . . . suicidal risks . . . (*She sits staring absently into space.*) That's right. (*As if to herself.*) . . . somer-
saults . . . hard to believe now (*in a faraway voice*) . . . there
was one somersault called the leap of death . . . I remember
a little girl . . . the gypsies taught her how to do the leap of
death . . . on a green green meadow near our cottage when I
was a little girl . . . I can hardly believe I ever was a little
girl . . . (*She imitates her mother's voice calling her in from
play.*)—Lili! Lili!—my mother was dead scared of those gypsies; she was sure they were going to up sticks and carry me
off. (*Coming to herself again.*) Well, I didn't get kidnapped,
and eventually I too learnt to do the leap of death all by
myself. Moving from the country to the city made a regular
contortionist of me. The deeper you get into this false, artificial world, the more false and artificial it becomes. There's
no way out. If you try to recreate simplicity in yourself or
around you on purpose it simply doesn't ring true—how can
it?—it's a fake, it isn't true. Nothing is true any more . . . All
I want is to see and to feel that there is one thing, just one
thing about me which is true!

DORO: But what about the hidden goodness inside the real
you? The goodness I tried to explain to people . . . ?

DELIA: Oh, yes; and I'm very grateful, but it's all so complicated, complicated . . . I mean the very fact that your efforts
made them angry, made them laugh. You explained it to me,
too, remember? You explained how I had this rotten reputation, how the people in Capri didn't want to know me. (I
believe some of them even thought I was a spy.) And then I
made this fantastic discovery. I learnt what it means to 'love
people'. I 'love people', people say; do you know what that
means? It means being pleased with yourself. When you're
pleased with yourself you go around 'loving people'. And
that's how he was, lucky old Giorgio, full of philanthropic

spirit, when he arrived in Capri after a highly successful exhibition of his paintings in Naples . . .

DORO: Giorgio Salvi?

DELIA: . . . an exhibition of landscapes. He was still euphoric when we met in Capri.

DORO: I guessed as much. Completely wrapped up in his painting with no time for finer feelings.

DELIA: Everything was colour with him! By then even feelings were colours.

DORO: And he wanted you to sit for him . . .

DELIA: That was the beginning. And you know, he had this awful way of asking for things. Like a spoilt child. So I became his model. And then it was as you said. There is nothing more irritating than being excluded from somebody's secret joy . . .

DORO: . . . particularly when it is being shoved at you left, right and centre and you have no idea as to what it's all about . . .

DELIA: Too right! I was a joy to him, a source of visual bliss for him alone. It wasn't a joy I could share. And in the end you see it meant that just like everybody else, all he wanted from me was my body. He was better than the others; he wasn't lusting after it, but still, the body was the thing.

DORO: And in the long run, this would be extra-maddening . . .

DELIA: Oh, yes! All those chaps I went running round to, desperate for reassurance, they all had such one-track minds that all I ever felt was nausea and contempt. This was a subtler disgust. Giorgio only wanted the body, too, but for a different kind of pleasure . . .

DORO: . . . an ideal pleasure . . .

DELIA: . . . but which left me out in the cold! . . .

DORO: . . . left you, rather, burning with added indignation and done out of your pretext for physical disgust.

DELIA: There was no way of getting back at him! With the others I could at least get my revenge. For a woman, an angel is far more infuriating to deal with than a brute beast!

DORO (beaming): Well, well! The very words I used! My own actual words.

DELIA: I know! I am using your words! As they were told to me. They make everything so clear.

DORO: So, until I explained it . . .

DELIA: I didn't know why I had done it! But you were quite right! It was for revenge! I deliberately set about bringing my body to life. I saw to it that very gradually the appeal became more than merely visual.

DORO: . . . and as soon as you saw that you had got him, that like the others he was well and truly hooked, then, as a refinement of revenge, you denied him any pleasure he might ask of your body beyond the purely visual one, which up till then had satisfied him . . .

DELIA: Oh, yes, he was above the needs of ordinary mortals!

DORO: All right! I'm with you! So your vengeance was complete! I mean, you didn't want him to marry you, did you?

DELIA: Heavens, no! I did all I possibly could to put him off! I refused him and refused him and in the end he was quite desperate and threatening to do all sorts of rash and silly things. Then I just wanted to clear off altogether.

DORO: That was when you started imposing impossible conditions on him, knowing they were impossible . . .

DELIA: Oh, I knew, I knew . . .

DORO: You insisted on being introduced to his mother and sister as his official fiancée . . .

DELIA: . . . yes, yes, well, he was fantastically proud and protective about his irreproachable and unapproachable family. The idea was to get him to say no! God, the way he went on about that younger sister!

DORO: Fine! That is precisely what I said! So, what happened exactly? When the sister's fiancé, Michele Rocca . . .

DELIA (*shuddering*): Don't even say his name! Please, I can't bear it!

DORO: This bit now is the crux of it. This will really prove I got it right. You must tell me I got this next bit right.

DELIA: . . . Yes, all right, I went off with him. In sheer desperation I went off with him, as the only possible way out.

DORO: So I was right! That is—terrific!

DELIA: The whole idea was to be discovered, to get Giorgio to find us together . . . as the only way of escaping that dreadful marriage . . .

DORO: . . . which, after all, would only have made him miserable . . .

DELIA: . . . and me! It would have made me miserable too! . . .

DORO (*triumphant*): So there we have it! I was right, all along
the line! This was my defence! And that idiot Francesco said
I had got it wrong. He made out that you were manipulating
Giorgio, that it was all a deadly plot to catch him . . .

DELIA (*shaken*): Francesco said that?

DORO: . . . that by refusing him, and arguing with him, and
making him suicidal, and threatening to clear off, you were
just getting him more and more desperate. You manoeuvred
his infatuation . . .

DELIA (*still shaken*): Francesco said that!

DORO: Oh yes . . . and that afterwards you played on his desperation by refusing him, as a way of getting him to agree to
all sorts of unthinkable conditions . . .

DELIA (*overwhelmed with shock*): What conditions?

DORO: Well, mainly the introduction to the mother and the
sister and the sister's fiancé.

DELIA: He didn't see that that was an attempt to stop the
marriage by getting Giorgio to say no?

DORO: No, he reckoned it was all part of another vile plot . . .

DELIA: What plot?

DORO: He reckoned what you wanted was to flaunt your vic-
tory, to cut a figure in society, side by side with the pure little
sister . . . after the humiliation of being treated like dirt . . .

DELIA (*mortified*): Did he say that? (*She looks crushed,
stunned.*)

DORO: He certainly did! And he said that when you heard the
reason for the delay over the introduction, that it was Michele
Rocca, the sister's fiancé, who was against it . . .

DELIA: He thought I was getting back at Rocca?

DORO: Precisely, another vile plot!

DELIA: I was punishing Rocca for not wanting to meet me?

DORO: That's right. You went to work on Rocca and ensnared
him in your toils, with never a thought for Salvi, intent on
showing the precious sister just what all this rigid respect-
ability and unsullied virtue add up to! (DELIA *is silent for a*

long time, staring into space as if deprived of sense. Then she suddenly buries her face in her hands and stays like this for several seconds.)

DORO (*after staring at her in puzzled astonishment*): What is it? (DELIA *is slow to uncover her face.*)

DELIA (*finally looking up and staring in front of her, then spreading out her hands in a desolate gesture.*) Who knows? Who knows? Perhaps that's right. Perhaps that is why I did it.

DORO (*astonished*): What? Well . . . if that's so . . . (*At this point* DONNA LIVIA *comes into the inner room, calling out in a state of extreme agitation.*)

DONNA LIVIA: Doro! Doro!

DORO (*leaping up at the urgent note in her voice*): Mother! What is it?

DONNA LIVIA (*hurrying in*): Doro! While I was out people told me that yesterday's scandal has become an affair of honour. Savio is demanding satisfaction.

DORO: Good Lord, no! Who said that?

DONNA LIVIA (*casting her eyes on* DELIA, *with contempt*): Do I actually find this person in my house?

DORO (*slowly, with emphasis*): Indeed, Mother, you do. In, as you say, your house.

DELIA: I'm going. I'm going. There won't be a duel. Don't worry Donna Livia, there won't be a duel. I shall stop it. I shall find a way of stopping it. (*She hurries away in evident distress*).

DORO (*making to go after her*): Miss Morello, please don't do anything rash! Don't try to interfere! (DELIA *has gone*).

DONNA LIVIA (*calling after him to stop him following*): So it's true?

DORO (*shouting back at her in exasperation*): What's true? That I am going to fight? I might. Though God knows why. Over a question which nobody can answer. I don't know the truth about it. Nor does Savio. She doesn't even know herself! She doesn't even know herself!

CURTAIN

FIRST CHORAL INTERLUDE

*The curtain rises again, immediately after being lowered at the
end of* ACT ONE, *revealing a section of the corridor which
encircles the auditorium. There are doors leading to the stalls
and boxes. Members of the audience emerge from these doors,
having just seen the first act. Others are presumably emerging
from the corresponding passage on the far side of the house,
off-stage, and some of these in fact wander in at intervals from
stage left.*

*The device of presenting part of the theatre foyer on stage,
and of peopling it with audience members who have supposedly
just watched the first act, will have a distancing effect upon the
events of the play. Relegated to a second plane, they will lose
the impact of real-life incidents and take on the perspective of
fictional invention. Later, at the end of the first choral interlude,
this passage with its members of the 'audience' will in turn be
distanced to a third plane as realisation dawns that the play on
the stage is a 'pièce à clef': intentionally based on a case said
to be drawn from real life and much publicised by the press: the
notorious 'Moreno' case, involving the suicide of Giacomo la
Vela and linking the names of Amelia Moreno and Baron Nuti.
Once it is known that La Moreno and Nuti are in fact present
in the audience tonight, another level of reality will be estab-
lished, right in the foreground and close to real life, rendering
somewhat irrelevant the heated arguments of those who have
attacked the play on purely artistic grounds. In the second
choral interlude all three planes will collide and conflict as the
characters of the real-life drama attack the fictive ones in the
play and the 'audience' attempts to intervene. The performance
will not, after this, be able to take place.*

*Meanwhile this first choral interlude must be played with
maximum naturalism, chattiness, fluidity and vivacity. The routine is by now familiar: the inevitable arguments and fric-
tion which fill the intervals of Pirandello's irritating plays. My
advice to his supporters is: treat those intractable opponents to
a display of smiling deference; it will be splendidly effective in
exacerbating their spleen.*

At first these 'audience' members will be in groups; people will hop about from one group to another in search of enlightenment. Part of the fun will be the reversals of opinion that take place, certain individuals changing their view two or even three times after overhearing two or three conflicting viewpoints. Here and there a placid spectator will be smoking; if he's bored he will be puffing away at his boredom; if he's puzzled, he will be puffing over his perplexity. The trouble with smoking is that like most vices, once it becomes a habit, sadly it hardly ever induces pleasure in itself, but simply takes on the flavour of the moment and the mood in which it is indulged. Those who are finding the play irritating may smoke too, if they wish, and convert their irritation into smoke.

The uniforms of two policemen may be glimpsed in the crowd; also uniformed attendants, programme sellers, and usherettes in black dresses and white aprons. A newsvendor threads his way through, shouting his headlines. There are a few ladies among the various groups, not smoking, one hopes, but one cannot of course be sure. Others appear and disappear through the doors leading to the boxes, using the interval to visit friends.

The five drama critics are at first reluctant to give an opinion, especially if expressly asked for one. Gradually they get together to exchange impressions. Blatant eavesdroppers attach themselves to their circle, attracting more and more attention from the curious, until the critics either clam up entirely or drift away among the crowd. They are quite capable of tearing the play and the author to shreds here in the foyer, and of giving a favourable account of both in their paper tomorrow morning. (A man is never to be identified with his profession; his profession may well exact a sacrifice of his sincerity, assuming, of course, that he has some sincerity to sacrifice.) And just so may the spectators who applauded with enthusiasm at the end of Act One be its most savage critics during the interval.

It would be perfectly possible to entrust the entire first choral interlude to improvisation, the range of possible comments on this author being familiar to everyone by now, and known to be equally applicable to all and any of his plays: 'cerebral', for instance, and 'paradoxical', 'obscure', 'absurd', and 'non-realistic'. However,

*the following dialogue indicates the essential points to be
covered by the actors who now briefly hold the stage. The
scripted dialogue may be supplemented by bona fide improvisation to increase the sense of confusion and excitement.*

*The first sound we hear is a buzz consisting of the brief
exclamations, questions, and perfunctory answers of those who
have been bored by the play and so are the first to emerge. The
rumble of continuing applause may be heard from inside the
auditorium. Two people emerge in some haste.*

FIRST HASTY PERSON: I'll pop upstairs and find him!
SECOND HASTY PERSON: Second row of the dress circle,
    about eight seats in! Mind you tell him, now!
FIRST HASTY PERSON: Don't worry! Leave it to me!
MAN (*entering from left*): Ah! You got in, then!
FIRST HASTY PERSON: As you see! I'm sorry, I've got to
    dash! (*He rushes off. More people enter from the left. A good
    deal of chatter is heard coming from this direction. Still more
    people emerge from the stalls and boxes.*)
ANYONE: Nice full house!
SOMEONE ELSE: Fantastic! Absolutely fantastic!
A THIRD: Have you seen them at all?
A FOURTH: I don't think they're here.

*In the hum of chatter one can pick out various greetings, plen-
tiful 'good-evenings', snatches of disconnected conversation,
introductions. A circle forms of the author's admirers, recogniz-
able by their bright eyes and animated expressions, who seek
each other out to exchange first impressions. Later they split up
and join other groups in order to speak up for the author and
his play, some of them petulantly, some ironically, defending
him against the uncompromising attacks of his adversaries, who
have similarly sought each other out.*

ADMIRERS OF THE PLAY: Hey! We're over here!
    Well, what did you think?
    It's going awfully well, isn't it?
    Ouf! That's better! Breath of air!

That last scene, with the woman!

She was certainly something, wasn't she?

The scene where the two changed sides worked well, I thought.

THE OPPOSITION: So . . . the usual Pirandello rigmarole! What's he trying to do?

Make the audience look silly!

I think what it is, he's getting much too confident.

I couldn't understand a word they said!

I think that's intentional.

As entertainment, I reckon it's a pain.

ONE OF PIRANDELLO'S ATTACKERS (*to the group of admirers*): Well, you lot, what's it all about then, eh?

SECOND ATTACKER (*aside*): Oh my God! Here come the experts!

ONE OF THE ADMIRERS: Are you asking me?

FIRST ATTACKER: No dear, I was asking our friend here. (*He indicates one of their group.*)

CHOSEN SPOKESMAN: Ah, you're asking me?

FIRST ATTACKER: Yes I was, though God knows why; you don't know the first thing about the theatre!

CHOSEN SPOKESMAN: Whereas you, who do, dismiss this kind of play as rubbish, don't you? You just shrug it off!

VOICES FROM A NEARBY GROUP: But what is there to understand, for heaven's sake?

You didn't get it either?

Nobody can make head or tail of it.

Well, it just seems to be: that first they say one thing and then they say the opposite. So what?

It's a joke!

And what was all that speechifying at the beginning?

Yes, where did that get us?

EAVESDROPPER (*moving from one group to another*): It's a joke. No one can make head or tail of it.

VOICES FROM ANOTHER GROUP: You can't say it's not interesting!

But it's so stale! This endless harping on the same old theme!

But I don't think he is!

But it's a whole way of looking at life! A whole way of perceiving!

Yes, well, he has made his point now, hasn't he? Perhaps it is time he just shut up!

I think it is. People are getting awfully sick of it.

But you clapped . . . You did! I saw you!

But surely . . . surely a view of life can have several facets if it is to be a total view of life!

But what is his view of life? Can you tell me what that first act was all about? Did it make sense to you?

Good question. But then, perhaps it wasn't supposed to make sense! And that's the point. What we have here is a play which shows that feelings and opinions do not make sense.

EAVESDROPPER (*moving to another group*): Got it! Fine! That's it! It's not supposed to make sense! This is the point! What we have here is a play that does not make sense!

VOICES FROM A THIRD GROUP (*hanging round the professional critics*): Seems like rubbish to me!

What are we supposed to make of it?

Let's ask the critics! Perhaps the professionals can enlighten us!

FIRST PROFESSIONAL CRITIC: Patchy, I thought. Bit of cutting might help.

QUESTIONER FROM THE GROUP: What was all that stuff about conscience?

SECOND CRITIC: Well, hold on! We've only seen one act!

THIRD CRITIC: Ye-es, but in all fairness, I'm not sure it's really on, this business of doing away with character. I mean, can you just let the action wander about all over the place? Can you base an entire drama on a disagreement, plucked out of the air like that?

FOURTH CRITIC: But the disagreement arises from the drama; it is the drama.

SECOND CRITIC: If you're looking for drama, well, I think the woman says it all, really.

THIRD CRITIC: I'd be quite happy to see the drama just acted out straightforwardly in the form of a play.

AN ADMIRER OF THE PLAY: The woman's a stroke of genius!

AN ATTACKER: You mean the girl playing her* is a genius.

EAVESDROPPER (*returning to the group he was with first of all*): If you're looking for drama, I think the woman says it all really. No doubt about it. At least we all agree about that. She's a stroke of genius.

MEMBER OF THE FIRST GROUP: Oh, come off it! It's just a jumble of conflicting propositions.

ANOTHER: He's an inveterate casuist, isn't he? I must say, I find it unbearably tedious.

A THIRD: It's a maze of logical tripwires. Just mental gymnastics, really.

EAVESDROPPER (*returning to the second group*): I have to say, he's an inveterate casuist, he really is. Everyone agrees with me.

FOURTH PROFESSIONAL CRITIC (*to the* THIRD): But look at the characters, for heaven's sake. They are hardly the sort of people one's going to meet in real life!

THIRD CRITIC: They are mouthpieces, of course! Just there to say the words.

FOURTH CRITIC: Ironic, really, using words to point out the inefficacy of language.

FIFTH CRITIC: What worries me is the misuse of theatre. Theatre, where possible, should be Art . . .

ONE OF THE ATTACKERS: Quite right! It should be poetic. What is missing here is any element of poetry.

FIFTH CRITIC: . . . So is it proper, I wonder, to use it for debate! Splendid stuff, I don't say it isn't—but is the theatre really the place to bandy arguments?

AN ADMIRER OF THE PLAY: If you ask me the argument is all going on out here. I didn't notice any on the stage. All I could hear was the quite unreasoning voice of suffering. If you call that argument . . .

ONE OF THE PLAY'S ATTACKERS: Let's ask the celebrated author. What do you make of it?

UNSUCCESSFUL OLD AUTHOR: M'mm . . . Well, all I can say is, if you like it you can keep it. You know my view.

---

* *Translator's note:* It is possible here, in performance, to substitute the name of the actress playing the part of Delia Morello.

VOICES: Come on! Tell us your view! We want to hear it!

UNSUCCESSFUL OLD AUTHOR: These are just paltry cerebral preoccupations, my friends . . . it's just a load of . . . well . . . what shall I say? fiddling little philosophical riddles not worth the paper they are written on!

FOURTH CRITIC: I really can't agree with that!

UNSUCCESSFUL OLD AUTHOR (*with increasing pomposity*): There's no depth, no spiritual crisis, no conviction, because there's no spontaneous emotional driving-force.

FOURTH CRITIC: Ah, now we're on familiar ground. Spiritual crisis and emotional driving-force are old friends!

LITERARY MAN (*who does not write*): But there's no real artistic subtlety is there? I mean, any of us could write this sort of stuff.

FOURTH CRITIC: Personally I'd like to reserve judgement. I can see it has the odd spark, the occasional flash of something. I feel a bit sort of dazed actually, as if I had seen the whole thing in a crazy distorting mirror.

From the right comes a tumultuous roar of angry voices. There are shouts of 'Lock him up!', 'He's off his chump!', 'The man's deranged!', and 'Swindle!', 'Rip-off', 'Give us our money back!' People crowd onto the stage asking, 'Whatever's going on out there?'

IRRITATED SPECTATOR: Does all hell have to break loose every time there's a Pirandello first night?

PLACID SPECTATOR: Let's hope they don't get violent!

ONE OF THE PLAY'S ADMIRERS: You should realise how lucky you are! When you go to plays by other writers, you settle down in your seat and allow yourself to be carried away by the make-believe world on the stage. (Well, that's what happens when it works.) But when you come to a Pirandello play you grip the arms of your chair like this and hold your head ready to butt back the words the author sends you. You hear a word, any word . . . say, chair! Got it? Pirandello says 'chair'. But oh, no! You can't fool me so easily. When Pirandello says 'chair' you don't know what you are going to find!

ONE OF THE OPPONENTS: You certainly don't! I can tell you what you won't find though, and that's poetry!

OTHERS: He's right! He's right! That's what is missing! That's what we want! Some poetry!

ANOTHER PIRANDELLO SUPPORTER: You can have your poetry! There are plenty of lesser writers whose little chairs are stuffed with it.

OTHER OPPONENTS: Well, I'm sick to death of the angst and the nihilism! The wallowing in negativity! How can anything so negative be creative?

FIRST PIRANDELLO SUPPORTER (*lashing out*): Who's being negative? You're being negative!

ONE OF THOSE ADDRESSED: **We're** being negative? We've never suggested there's no such thing as reality!

FIRST SUPPORTER: Do you realise just who **is** denying your reality, such as it is?

SECOND SUPPORTER: You deny it yourself, every time you insist that that reality is one constant thing . . .

FIRST SUPPORTER: . . . the world as it seems to you at this moment . . .

SECOND SUPPORTER: . . . and forgetting that yesterday it looked quite different!

FIRST SUPPORTER: . . . because you accept your 'reality' at secondhand. You think the empty word 'reality' is like other words, like 'mountain', 'tree', or 'street'. You think it refers to a constant, given thing in itself. You feel cheated if somebody points out to you that it was just an illusion. How can you be so muddle-headed! This play is trying to show that each person has to make his own ground to stand on, a bit at a time, step by step. At each step the terrain changes; bits which are no longer relevant, which don't belong, crumble away. To go hankering off down memory lane after the old poetic dramas is parasitic! Parasitic! You can't tread firmly on a path you haven't made yourself!

BARON NUTI (*appearing from the left, pale, trembling, not himself, with two friends who try to restrain him*): And I'll tell you something else this play is trying to show! How to trample on the dead and discredit the living!

ONE OF HIS COMPANIONS (*gripping him firmly by the arm to lead him away*): No! Come on now! Come with me!

SECOND COMPANION (*at the same time*): Come on old chap! There's a good fellow! Come on!

BARON NUTI (*repeating in a shattered voice, as they drag him towards exit, left*): ... trample on the dead and discredit the living!

INQUISITIVE VOICES FROM THE CROWD (*amid a general murmur of astonishment*): Who's that? Who on earth's that? My God did you see his face? He looked like death! Do you think he's mad? Who is it for heaven's sake?

SOCIALITE: It's Baron Nuti ... Baron Nuti.

INQUISITIVE VOICES: Does anyone know him? Who is he? What was he talking about?

SOCIALITE: Heavens! Didn't you know? This is a *comédie à clef*.

ONE OF THE CRITICS: What's a *comédie à clef*?

SOCIALITE: It's based on real people! On the Moreno case! It's exactly the same! It has been lifted straight from life!

VOICES: The Moreno case?

Who's Moreno?

Amelia Moreno ... the actress ... You must have heard of her! She spent a long time in Germany ...

Everybody knows about her in Turin!

Oh, I know! The one in the suicide scandal ... La Vela wasn't it ... months ago ... did himself in ...

What the hell does Pirandello think he's up to?

But that's dreadful! Pirandello's writing about real people?

Well, yes! So it would seem!

He's done it before!

But can you base a work of art on real life?

As long as you don't do what the man said: trample on the dead and discredit the living.

Who's Nuti then?

SOCIALITE: Nuti's the one who caused the suicide. He's the chap who was going to marry La Vela's sister.

ANOTHER CRITIC: And did he really get off with La Moreno the night before the wedding?

ONE OF PIRANDELLO'S OPPONENTS: The cases are identical, then. I must say it's pretty gross.
ANOTHER OPPONENT: You mean the characters from the
real-life drama are here in the theatre?
A THIRD (*pointing off-stage*): There's Nuti, over there!
SOCIALITE: Moreno's up there, tucked away in a box. She
cottoned on at once. She went mad! She chewed three hand-
kerchiefs to shreds in the first act and they are making sure
she doesn't come down here. But I can't see her keeping
quiet. She'll make the most unholy row!
VOICES: Good for her! You can hardly blame her!
Think what a shock . . . seeing yourself in a play!
Having your private life paraded on the stage!
And the bloke! I found him quite terrifying!
Oh my God . . . I don't think I'm going to like this! (*Bells ring
to tell the audience to return to their seats.*)
There's the bell! There's the bell!
Time for Act Two!
Let's get back! Let's see what happens!

*There is a general movement back into the auditorium. A con-
fused murmur of rumour and comment is audible as the news
spreads. Three of those who have liked the play hang back and
are still on stage to see, in the now empty corridor, the arrival
of Moreno, who has come rushing down from her box. Three
friends are anxious to guide her away, out of the theatre and
out of harm's way. The theatre attendants look alarmed at first
but quickly make silencing gestures to stop her interrupting the
performance. The three Pirandello partisans stand back to ob-
serve; they are astonished and distressed by what now follows.*

MORENO: Stop it! Let me go! Let me go!
ONE OF HER FRIENDS: This is madness! What do you mean
to do?
MORENO: I'm going on stage!
SECOND FRIEND: For God's sake, why? Are you mad?
MORENO: Let go of me!
THIRD FRIEND: Come on! Let's get out of here!

THE OTHER TWO: Come on! Come on! We're going! Come on, love! You know it's best.

MORENO: Oh no, I don't! I've got to settle with this lot first! They can't be allowed to get away with it!

FIRST FRIEND: But what can you do? The theatre's full of people!

MORENO: I'll go on stage and show 'em.

SECOND FRIEND: You can't do that! Not while we're here to stop you!

MORENO: Let me go! I'm going up on that stage!

THIRD FRIEND: The actors are there already.

FIRST FRIEND: The second act has started?

MORENO (*suddenly calmer*): Has it? All right . . . I'll hear the rest of it, then . . . Let's go and hear the rest! (*She turns to go off left in the direction of her box.*)

HER FRIENDS: No, look! Let's go home! Come on now, it's the best thing to do! Come along!

MORENO (*insisting, dragging them with her*): No, we're going back. We are going back in! I've got to hear the rest of this, I've got to!

FIRST FRIEND (*as they go off, left*): But why torture yourself?

AN ATTENDANT (*to the three* PIRANDELLO SUPPORTERS *who have been watching all this*): What's got into them?

FIRST SUPPORTER: Do you see what's happening?

SECOND SUPPORTER: That was Moreno?

THIRD SUPPORTER: Just a moment . . . Is Pirandello backstage?

FIRST SUPPORTER: I'll tell him to disappear. We're in for disaster. I can feel it coming.

CURTAIN

ACT II

Francesco Savio's house, the following morning. A kind of gar-
den-room opening onto a spacious verandah, used by Savio for
fencing practice. Through the large French windows, which take
up most of the back wall, can be seen the fencing-piste, a long
bench for lookers-on, masks, gauntlets, jackets, foils and sabres.
Green curtains, hanging on large rings inside the French win-
dows, are sometimes used to shut off the view of the verandah
from the house. On the far side of the verandah a similar curtain
hangs from a metal frame affixed to the balustrade, protecting
the fencing-area from view on the garden side. Glimpses of the
garden appear when these curtains are parted to allow charac-
ters to leave the stage, supposedly via steps leading down to the
garden. The room is sparsely furnished with green wicker chairs,
two sunbeds, and two small tables, also of wicker. There is a
window to the left and an internal door to the right.
When the curtain rises FRANCESCO SAVIO *and his* FENC-
ING COACH *can be seen practising on the verandah, complete*
with masks, jackets and gloves. PRESTINO *and* TWO OTHER
FRIENDS *are watching.*

FENCING COACH: Open up! Invite an attack! Look out for
   your *dégagement*! Good! That's a nice *parry-quart*! Watch it!
   Parry! No need to keep inviting an attack, and stop making
   feints! Look out for the ripost! Stop! (*They lower their sabres.*
   The practise is over.) A well-timed retreat: that's it.
   (*They take off their masks.*)
FRANCESCO: That's enough. Thanks, Maestro. (*He shakes*
   his hand.)
PRESTINO: Yes, my goodness. That's enough.
FENCING COACH (*taking off his glove and then his jacket.*)
   You won't find it easy with Palegari. He's a man to think his
   tactics through in advance . . .
FIRST FRIEND: And he's an ace at stop-cuts. You'll have to
   watch out.
SECOND FRIEND: He's amazingly fast! And by fast, I mean
   fast!

FRANCESCO: I know, I know. (*He, too, removes glove and jacket.*)

FIRST FRIEND: You'll have to keep moving, keep out of range!

FENCING COACH: And don't take your eyes off his sabre for a second!

FRANCESCO: Yes, all right, all right.

SECOND FRIEND: The thing to do, if you can, is a downward lunge.

FIRST FRIEND: No, a stop-cut, a stop-cut is the best! Really! I know what I'm talking about. Let him run himself through!

FENCING COACH: But you're to be congratulated! That's a lovely *dégagement*!

PRESTINO: Just play it by ear and you'll be fine! Don't have a fixed plan. I expect you'll settle the whole thing with a cut on the glove. More to the point, hadn't we better drink to it? (*They all come into the garden room.*)

FRANCESCO: You're right, let's have a drink. (*He rings for the* BUTLER.) Well, Maestro, what will it be?

FENCING COACH: Oh, nothing for me. I don't drink in the morning.

FRANCESCO: I've a nice light ale.

PRESTINO: Sounds fine!

FIRST FRIEND: Certainly does! (*The* BUTLER *appears at the door on the right.*)

FRANCESCO: Bring us some light ale, will you? (*The* BUTLER *withdraws and returns with bottles and glasses on a tray. He serves them and leaves.*)

FIRST FRIEND: This must be the most farcical duel in history. You'll be dining out on it for months!

SECOND FRIEND: It must be the first time two people have fought a duel because each one thinks that the other one is right!

PRESTINO: But you can see how it could happen!

FIRST FRIEND: Can you? What do you mean?

PRESTINO: If you've got two people going in opposite directions and they suddenly turn round and decide to swop paths—well, they're going to crash into each other, aren't they?

FENCING COACH: That's what happened! The prosecution
    started defending and the defence started accusing! They
    even used each other's arguments!
FIRST FRIEND: Is that what happened?
FRANCESCO: I can honestly say I went round to his house in
    all good conscience . . .
FIRST FRIEND: You mean, it never crossed your mind that . . .
FRANCESCO: . . . I had only one thought in my head . . .
FIRST FRIEND: . . . and it never occurred to you that it might
    have been the most fearful gaffe to make that vicious attack
    on Delia Morello?
FRANCESCO: . . . Not for a moment . . .
FIRST FRIEND: Hang on a moment! . . . You're claiming total
    ignorance of the one feature of this case which to everybody
    else that evening was glaringly obvious? . . .
SECOND FRIEND: . . . that Doro was only defending her be-
    cause he is madly in love with her?
FRANCESCO: It didn't come into it! It was **because** I didn't
    think of it that we fell out! It never once crossed my mind,
    either then or later! How foolish one can look! And that's
    what people judge you by . . . it just takes one unthinking
    moment, one stupid false move . . . and you get all these ri-
    diculous repercussions. I had planned a nice little break for
    myself today; I'm supposed to be in the country staying with
    my sister and her husband.
PRESTINO: So your argument the night before last was a cool,
    considered discussion . . .
FRANCESCO: I was just looking at the case on its merits, I
    assure you! I had no idea of all these emotional undercurrents!
SECOND FRIEND: Doro really is in love with her, isn't he?
FIRST FRIEND: Oh, he's in love with her all right.
PRESTINO: Well, of course he is!
FRANCESCO: If I had any suspicion of this I should never
    have gone to his house like that to tell him he was right . . .
    bound to be touchy in the circumstances!
SECOND FRIEND (*with solemn emphasis*): Well, what I have
    to say is this! . . . Listen! . . . (*He breaks off and forgets what
    he has to say, while they wait eagerly for his pronouncement.*)

FIRST FRIEND (*after waiting a moment*): Well?

SECOND FRIEND: What I say . . . Oh, dear! . . . I don't remember. (DIEGO CINCI *appears in the doorway on the right.*)

DIEGO: May I come in?

FRANCESCO: Ah, Diego, it's you!

PRESTINO: Has somebody sent you?

DIEGO (*with a shrug*): Now who could have sent me? . . . Good morning, Maestro!

FENCING COACH: Good morning, Cinci. I'm actually just leaving. (*He shakes hands with* FRANCESCO SAVIO.) See you tomorrow, then, Savio! Not to worry, eh?

FRANCESCO: Thanks, I won't! And thanks for your help.

FENCING COACH (*to the others*): Good-bye, gentlemen. I'm sorry to leave such delightful company but I really do have to be off. (*The others nod good-bye.*)

FRANCESCO: Look, Maestro, you can go out this way. (*He shows him the door onto the verandah.*) Through the far curtain! The steps will take you down to the garden.

FENCING COACH: Thank you. Right. Good-day. Good-day. (*Exit*)

FIRST FRIEND (*to* DIEGO): We thought you would be Doro Palegari's second.

DIEGO (*making negative signs with index finger before speaking*): I didn't want to be. I was caught between the two of them yesterday. Friend of both, you see. I wanted to keep right out of it.

SECOND FRIEND: So what have you come for now?

DIEGO: To say how delighted I am about the duel!

PRESTINO: 'Delighted' is a bit strong isn't it? (*The others laugh.*)

DIEGO: A flesh wound each, I think, is what I'd recommend. Nothing too serious. Do them both good to lose a little blood. Something to show for it . . . nice little wound: two, three, anything up to five centimetres long. You know where you are with a nice scar. (*He takes* FRANCESCO *by the arm and turns back his sleeve a little.*) Look at your wrist. Not a mark. By tomorrow morning you will have a nice little incision there to look at!

FRANCESCO: Well, thanks! That's . . . most reassuring! (*The others laugh.*)

DIEGO (*breaking in*): Oh, and Doro, too! Don't let's be selfish! Doro must have one, too! Now, here's a surprise! Guess who turned up at Doro's after you left, after I ran after you to catch you up . . .

PRESTINO: . . . Not Delia Morello?

SECOND FRIEND: . . . to thank him for sticking up for her?

DIEGO: Well, yes. Except that . . . when she heard your arguments against her . . . do you know what she did?

FRANCESCO: What?

DIEGO: She said your accusations were justified.

FRANCESCO, PRESTINO AND FIRST FRIEND (*all at once*): She said what? . . . Good God! . . . And what did Doro say?

DIEGO: You can imagine how Doro felt!

SECOND FRIEND: He must be wondering what the devil he's fighting about!

FRANCESCO: Oh, he knows why he's fighting! He's fighting because of the insult, the fact he insulted me in front of you . . . when in point of fact I had gone round there, as you saw and as I was just explaining, expressly to tell him he was right.

DIEGO: So what now?

FRANCESCO: What do you mean, what now?

DIEGO: Now that you know that Delia Morello thinks **you** were right.

FRANCESCO: Ah, well . . . in that case . . . if she . . .

DIEGO: Oh, no! no! Francesco, dear fellow, you must carry on! She needs a champion more than ever, now! And you are the one to do it, her original accuser!

PRESTINO: Do you mean against her own self-accusations? Against her own original champion?

DIEGO: That's exactly what I do mean! She has gone up one hundred per cent in my estimation since she showed herself capable of this! (*He suddenly turns to* FRANCESCO.) Who are you? (*To* PRESTINO.) Who are you? Who am I? Who are any of us? Your name is Francesco Savio. Mine is Diego Cinci. Yours is Prestino. All we know of each other or of ourselves is the wretched crumb of certainty we seem to have today. It didn't apply yesterday and it won't apply tomorrow. (*To* FRANCESCO.) Now, you . . . you're a gentleman of leisure and you're bored out of your mind . . .

FRANCESCO: I am not! Whoever told you that?

DIEGO: Not bored? . . . Well, I'm glad to hear it. For myself, I spend my time burrowing like a mole into my own mind. My mind is now nothing but a mole-hole! What do you do, Prestino?

PRESTINO: Nothing, really.

DIEGO: A splendid profession, maybe the best! Because, you see, nobody's exempt from life's depredations. Even the people who work, the industrious upright majority, are all victims of life's endless smash and grab. Inwardly and outwardly it lays waste our substance. Stop, thief! Our most deeply-rooted affections are powerless against it, so what chance have the opinions, fantasies and ideas that we glimpse as we hurtle breathlessly along our frantic way! One new fact can shatter a previous opinion. In a flash white becomes black. A fleeting impression, a slight inflection of a voice, and you've changed your mind. To say nothing of the hundreds of images teeming in the mind itself which influence us subconsciously . . . You go for an evening walk and the road is getting dark. You're depressed. It's enough to lift your eyes to a balcony still warm and bright in the evening light and to notice a scarlet geranium glowing in the rays of the setting sun . . . and suddenly you are invaded by an indescribably tender and distant dream . . .

PRESTINO: What are you trying to prove?

DIEGO: Nothing. How can I? We can't prove things. That's the point. When you try to hold on to something stable and solid, all you've got is the miserable, boring, minute particle of certainty you have today; that mere fraction of yourself which is all you can ever really know of yourself: your name for instance, your address, the number of coins in your pocket: your daily routine, your likes and dislikes . . . the familiar round of your existence . . . oh, and your body of course, the poor old body still just about capable of movement and struggling along with the stream, until the day when it starts

to slow down and stiffen up with old age, getting stiffer and
stiffer and finally seizing up altogether, and time's up.

FRANCESCO: But I thought you were talking about Delia
Morello?

DIEGO: Indeed I was! . . . I was trying to explain the amazement, the joy, the rare and awesome joy of the wild moment
in the storm when we are suddenly knocked over by the mael-
strom and we see the silly little fabrications of our daily life
just crumble away; we see the flood swirling round us, roaring
over the dykes and embankments so carefully set up to contain
our consciousness, to constitute our personality. And then, the
bit we thought we knew, the tame familiar watercourse we
have so lovingly coaxed and channelled into neat systems of
affection, duty and habit—we stand by and watch that too
burst its banks in a magnificent cataclysmic deluge, destroying
and overturning everything in its wake. At last we have it, the
hurricane, the earthquake, the volcanic conflagration!

ALL (*together*): That's your idea of a good time is it,
Diego? . . . Great stuff, Diego, sounds terrific! . . . I think
I'll pass on this one . . . I find the idea entirely horrifying!

DIEGO: It is tragedy instead of farce. After the farce of all our
ridiculous choppings and changings we are faced at last with
tragedy, the plight of a soul in total disarray, the soul that is
completely flummoxed . . . And I don't mean just her! (*To*
FRANCESCO.) You'll see, Francesco, they'll descend on
you here, the pair of them! They'll land on your doorstep like
the wrath of God!

FRANCESCO: **They?** You don't mean Michele Rocca too?

DIEGO: Of course I mean Michele Rocca!

FIRST FRIEND: Oh, he's here! He got here from Naples last
night!

SECOND FRIEND: Oh, my God! that's what I meant to tell
you! Apparently he wants to challenge Palegari. He has been
going around looking for him!

PRESTINO: We knew about that. (*To* FRANCESCO.) I told
you, didn't I?

FRANCESCO (*to* DIEGO): I still don't see why he has got to
come and see me?

DIEGO: He wants to get at Palegari before you do! But now, don't you see, it's you he should be fighting!

FRANCESCO: Why me?

THE OTHERS: Yes why? What do you mean?

DIEGO: Well, obviously. You and Palegari have reversed roles haven't you? If you are quite serious about it you will have to answer for all the insulting allegations Doro made against Rocca at the Avanzis' the other night! It's clear enough: you are the one Rocca should be challenging now!

FRANCESCO: Hold on! Just a minute! What are you saying?

DIEGO: Look. You're fighting a duel with Doro because he insulted you, all right? Now why did he do that?

THE TWO FRIENDS (*breaking in*): I get it! Diego's right!

DIEGO: In a straight swap, you side with Delia Morello, and you attribute all blame to Michele Rocca.

PRESTINO (*shocked*): You're not serious about this!

DIEGO: Oh, I'm serious. (*To* FRANCESCO.) I even think that this time you can claim to be in the right.

FRANCESCO: So you want me to fight Michele Rocca as well?

DIEGO: No, I don't. That might have really serious consequences. Fighting with someone as desperate as that poor devil...

FIRST FRIEND: ... now that Salvi's death has put paid to any idea of his marrying the sister...

SECOND FRIEND: That marriage will certainly not take place...

DIEGO: ... discarded by Delia Morello...

FRANCESCO (*flaring up suddenly*): Discarded? Is that what you're saying now?

DIEGO: Well, she certainly made use of him...

FRANCESCO: ... played a rotten trick on him... as I said first of all...

DIEGO (*remonstrating, with a long-drawn-out syllable*): Hey! Watch it! You're in a bit of a fix and no doubt you're angry, but you really can't go changing your mind again!

FRANCESCO: I'm not changing my mind! Look, you said yourself that she admitted to Palegari that I was right, that what she did was a dirty trick!

DIEGO: You see? You see?

FRANCESCO: I'm damned if I do! When I learn that she admits she is guilty, of course I revert to my original opinion! (*Appealing to the others.*) It stands to reason doesn't it?

DIEGO: All right. She used Michele Rocca, I'll give you that. And yes, with him she certainly cheated. But the point is she did it to save Salvi from the disaster of marrying her. Don't you see? In no way was she betraying Salvi. It was solely for him that she did it. And on that score I'll defend her to the hilt, against her own protestations of guilt if necessary; yes . . . I would even defend her against herself!

FRANCESCO (*annoyed, but giving in*): All right. All right. Swayed by the famous arguments of Doro Palegari . . .

DIEGO: . . . the very same arguments, mind . . .

FRANCESCO: Don't say it, I know! The very same arguments which changed my mind the first time. All right! But there's no getting round her betrayal of Rocca!

DIEGO: She was a woman. Perhaps that's all that can be said. Along he came, apparently looking for a good time with no strings, and that's exactly what she gave him. There's nothing the matter with Michele Rocca except hurt male pride! He can't face the fact that in this case a woman has used him as a sort of toy, had her fun and cast him aside. He was her doll; a stuffed clown which she simply smashed in pieces once she had tired of playing with it, opening and shutting its arms in attitudes of prayer, pressing a button in its chest to make it squeak with passion. Well, now the stuffed clown has picked himself up. His poor little china face and hands are ruined and his fingers are all snapped off; the nose is gone and the face is badly chipped and cracked; the spring which worked the squeak has broken; it is sticking out of his chest through a hole in the red satin waistcoat. But the stuffed clown is protesting now. 'No!' he cries, 'It wasn't like that! That's not what happened at all! It's not true that she made me do all those things to make fun of me! She didn't open and shut my arms and batter me to bits! It's not true!' A touching picture don't you think?

PRESTINO (*losing his temper and raising clenched fists*): How can you make fun of something like that! It's not a joke!

DIEGO (*unperturbed, while the others are shocked*): Did I say it was?

PRESTINO: You treat everything as a joke. From the moment you came in you've been trying to make us all look ridiculous—Francesco, me, everyone!

DIEGO: Dear idiot—I'm ridiculous myself!

PRESTINO: You are the idiot, with your facile laughter! You treat us like toy windmills . . . You know, you blow on them and make them turn in any direction you like. I can't bear to hear him talk! What must his soul be like? You know how ersatz dye rots cloth? Well, I imagine Diego's soul all burnt away by the caustic action of his talk.

DIEGO: You've got it wrong, dear boy. I laugh because . . .

PRESTINO: . . . because you have hollowed out your heart. You said so yourself. You said it was a mole-hole. There is nothing in your heart, and that is why you laugh.

DIEGO: You may think so.

PRESTINO: Oh, I think so all right. And even if what you say is true and human beings are as changeable as you say, then that strikes me as sad, not funny, and people should be pitied.

DIEGO (*angry, too, now, grasping* PRESTINO *by both shoulders and staring closely into his face*): Oh, yes! To be pitied indeed when looked at like this!

PRESTINO: Like what?

DIEGO: Like this, eye to eye. No . . . look at me! Look at me as you are, stripped to the skin and complete with all the wretchedness and rotteness you have inside you—oh yes, I'm no different!—all the fears, regrets and inconsistencies. Throw out the stuffed clown, the dummy version you concoct to make sense of your actions and feelings . . . throw him out and you will find that he has nothing whatever in common with what you really are and what you can be, and with what is there inside you yet to be discovered. For what you have in there is a god—terrible, if thwarted—but unfailingly merciful if you give in and admit failure. Oh yes, it will feel like treachery; you'll think you're letting yourself down as a man. This is what comes of equating our humanity with notions like conscience, and consistency, and courage. But were you being more human the one time you practised courage? Or the dozen times you were frightened and disposed to act with prudence? You have agreed to act as Savio's second in this stupid duel with Palegari. (*To* SAVIO.) And you thought that yesterday when Palegari called you an idiot that he meant . . . you. He didn't mean you. He meant himself. You didn't realise it, but he was really talking to the dummy he was unable to perceive in himself but which he could see mirrored in you. I admit to laughing, but what else can I do? I'm always the first victim of my own laughter. (*There is a pause. They are all absorbed by their separate trains of thought. The following exchange is punctuated by pauses, each one speaking as if to himself*).

FRANCESCO: Well, of course, I have no real quarrel with Doro Palegari. He dragged me into it . . .

PRESTINO (*after another pause*): So often in life we have to put on a show of certainty. If the pretence costs us dear, I'd say we are all the more to be pitied!

FIRST FRIEND (*after another pause, as if reading* FRANCE-SCO SAVIO's *thoughts*): I bet it's glorious in the country today!

FRANCESCO (*not surprised at having his train of thought shared; his tone almost apologetic*): Oh, dear, and I had even bought some toys to take to my small niece.

SECOND FRIEND: What an enchanting child she was! Is she still?

FRANCESCO: More so if anything. She's lovely. Angelic. I've never known anything like her. (*He gets a clockwork teddy-bear out of its package winds it up, and puts it through its paces on the floor. They all laugh at the performance and then fall silent, oddly cheerless.*)

DIEGO (*to* FRANCESCO): Listen. If I were you . . . (*He is interrupted by the* BUTLER *who appears in the doorway, right.*)

BUTLER: Excuse me, sir.

FRANCESCO: What is it?

BUTLER: May I have a word with you, sir? (*FRANCESCO goes over to him and hears what he has to say. The BUTLER's words are inaudible.*)

FRANCESCO: Oh, no. Now, do you mean? (*He turns, nonplussed, to look at his friends, uncertain what to do or say.*)

DIEGO (*realising what has happened*): She's here, isn't she?

PRESTINO: You can't receive her! You really must not!

FIRST FRIEND: That's right! Not before the duel!

DIEGO: Rubbish! The duel has nothing to do with her!

PRESTINO: It has! She is the cause of it! Oh, no! . . . in fact, as your representative, I am forbidding you to receive her.

SECOND FRIEND: You can't send a lady away just like that, without even finding out what she has come for!

DIEGO: I am staying out of this.

FIRST FRIEND (*to FRANCESCO*): You could just hear . . .

SECOND FRIEND: Yes, and then if she . . .

FRANCESCO: If she starts talking about the duel . . . ?

PRESTINO: Just cut her short! Send her packing!

FRANCESCO: I'm quite happy to send her packing anyway!

PRESTINO: All right. Never mind. Go on. Go and see her. (*Exit FRANCESCO followed by the BUTLER.*)

DIEGO: My only stipulation would be that he should tell her . . . (*He is interrupted by the sudden entrance of MICHELE ROCCA, who comes bursting in from the garden, flinging aside the verandah curtains in fury. He is clearly in the grip of some horrific barely-contained frenzy. He is about thirty years old, dark, haggard, his face ravaged by passion and remorse. His expression and bearing are those of a man who will stop at nothing*).

ROCCA: May I come in? (*He is clearly surprised at finding so many people here.*) Have I come to the right house?

PRESTINO (*expressing the astonishment they are all feeling*): Who are you, pray?

ROCCA: Michele Rocca.

DIEGO: Ah, Michele Rocca.

ROCCA (*to DIEGO*): Are you Francesco Savio?

DIEGO: No Savio's through there. (*Nodding in the direction of the door, right.*)

PRESTINO: How did you manage to come in this way?

ROCCA: I was told this was the way in.

DIEGO: The concierge probably thought he was a friend ...

ROCCA: Has a lady just called at this house?

PRESTINO: Why, were you following her?

ROCCA: I certainly was following her. And I knew that this was where she would come.

DIEGO: So did I! And I knew that you would come!

ROCCA: Terrible things have been said about me, I know. I also know that Signor Savio, without even knowing me, has spoken up on my behalf. I have to tell him, I simply have to tell him not to listen to anything that woman says until I've had a chance to explain to him what the situation really is.

PRESTINO: Signor Rocca, I'm sorry, but you have come too late!

ROCCA: Too late? What do you mean?

PRESTINO: Nothing you can do now will stop it!

FIRST FRIEND: The challenge has been accepted ...

SECOND FRIEND: Conditions have been agreed ...

DIEGO: ... and minds radically changed!

PRESTINO (*angrily to* DIEGO): You can shut up, Diego! Just keep out of this and stay out.

FIRST FRIEND: He does it on purpose! He likes to make things as difficult as he can!

DIEGO: That's hardly fair! Signor Rocca came here thinking Savio was his ally. I'm just letting him know that this is no longer the case.

ROCCA: What—do you mean he has joined the prosecution!

DIEGO: He's not alone in that!

ROCCA: And you? Which side are you on?

DIEGO: I, too, side with the prosecution. All of us here, in fact, as you probably can see.

ROCCA: Yes ... I bet you do! You've only heard her side of it!

DIEGO: But we haven't! We've none of us heard her side of it! Nor has Savio. He is through there now, just meeting her for the first time.

ROCCA: So how are you so sure I am in the wrong? Even Signor Savio who took my side? And why, if he's changed his mind, does he still want to fight Palegari?

DIEGO: Signor Rocca, you probably think of madness . . . well, I expect you think of madness as something . . . well, grotesque and extreme, but . . . as I was saying earlier . . . we're all a bit touched with madness. These two, if you must know, are fighting because they have both changed their minds about you.

FIRST FRIEND (*interrupting, the others supporting him*): Don't listen to him! It's not true!

SECOND FRIEND: They are fighting because after the fracas on the first evening Palegari lost his temper . . .

FIRST FRIEND: . . . and hurled abuse at Savio . . .

PRESTINO: . . . and Savio took offence and challenged Palegari . . .

DIEGO (*raising his voice above them all*): . . . although everybody by then agreed . . .

ROCCA (*abruptly and vehemently*): . . . to put all the blame on me without even listening to my case? But how has that diabolical woman got all you lot onto her side like this?

DIEGO: All of us, that is . . . except herself.

ROCCA: Except herself?

DIEGO: Well, what shall I say . . . You must not think that she is on one side or the other. She's not too sure which side she's on. And if you take a long, hard look at yourself, Signor Rocca, you won't know which side you're on either.

ROCCA: Well, there's nothing like a nice bit of fun . . . I wonder if somebody would be kind enough to tell Signor Savio that I am here!

PRESTINO: But what have you got to say to him? I told you, it's too late!

ROCCA: How can you know? If he's against me now, then all the more reason to see him!

PRESTINO: Just now he is with Signorina Morello.

ROCCA: Better still! In fact I followed her here. And maybe it's quite lucky for her that we are meeting here like this, in semi-public, in the house of a total stranger quite unconnected with our case. Because . . . God! I was in a mood to stop at nothing! I . . . couldn't even see where I was going . . .

and . . . now, well, finding myself in this room like this, with
all these people making me talk and asking me questions . . .
I don't know . . . I feel . . . sort of . . . well, relaxed somehow
and sort of lighter. It's been days since I had anyone to talk
to. I can't describe to you people what it has been like! . . .
Well, as near to hell as may be . . . And it was all to save my
friend! . . . he would have been my brother-in-law . . . I loved
him like a brother . . .

PRESTINO: You tried to save him? You amaze me!

FIRST FRIEND: . . . carrying off the bride . . . ?

SECOND FRIEND: . . . on the eve of the wedding . . . ?

ROCCA: No! Let me explain! I never carried off the bride! It
wasn't like that! It didn't take much to save Giorgio! It was
simply a matter of giving him tangible proof that he didn't
actually have to marry the girl in order to have her. He could
have her without marrying her, as anybody could, and lots of
people did.

PRESTINO: Nevertheless, you took her from him.

ROCCA: He bet me I couldn't!

FIRST FRIEND: What!

SECOND FRIEND: Who bet you?

ROCCA: Giorgio did! I'll tell you. The mother and the sister
backed me. After they had met Delia (Poor Giorgio! That
must have offended his sense of the proprieties, introducing
such a woman to his family!), well, after they met her, the
mother, the sister and I planned the whole thing. I joined
Giorgio and Delia down in Naples, ostensibly to help them
with their new house. The wedding was to be in a few months.
One day they had a row, a lovers' squabble of sorts, and off
she went in a huff and stayed away for several days. (*He
covers his eyes with his hands as if suddenly struck by a
horrific image.*) God! I've got the clearest picture of her
leaving . . . (*He uncovers his eyes.*) I was there, you see, when
they quarrelled. (*Recovering*) Well, this was my moment to
show Giorgio what a mad idea the marriage was. It was an
incredible set-up! Incredible! For instance, she did this thing
those women often do, of, well, witholding her favours as
they say—but totally! . . .

FIRST FRIEND (*fascinated, as they all are*): Typical!

ROCCA: . . . and at Capri she had been extremely aloof and superior, treating everybody else like dirt. So, it was a bet! He bet me I couldn't do it! He bet me I could not produce proof of what I was trying to tell him. His part of the bargain was, that if I could prove it to him he would give her up, break it off. Instead of which, he killed himself.

FIRST FRIEND: You lent yourself to this mad scheme?

ROCCA: He had challenged me! And the point was to save him!

SECOND FRIEND: So who betrayed whom?

ROCCA: It's awful! . . . awful!

SECOND FRIEND: In effect he betrayed you!

ROCCA: Yes, he did! Yes, he did!

SECOND FRIEND: By killing himself!

PRESTINO: It's unbelievable! It is completely unbelievable!

ROCCA: What's unbelievable? That I should have agreed to the bet?

PRESTINO: No! . . . that he should have let you go to such extremes to prove your point!

ROCCA: He knew what he was doing! He had seen her at work. From the moment she first saw me—and don't forget, I was Giorgio's sister's fiancé— she had made a dead-set at me. Out of sheer bitchiness. She tried every damn trick in the book . . . In fact it was Giorgio who pointed it out! So that it was the most natural thing in the world for me to say 'Look Giorgio, you know that given half a chance she would even hop into bed with me!'

PRESTINO: Good God! in a sense he was challenging himself!

ROCCA: He should have shouted in my face! He should have made me see how deeply the poison had got into him! He was well and truly hooked! Removing the viper's fangs now wasn't going to do any good.

DIEGO (*interrupting*): Look you really can't go calling her a viper!

ROCCA: Oh, she's a viper! Make no mistake about that!

DIEGO: Not quite calculating enough for a viper, I'd have said. It was all so quick! Look at the speed with which she sank her fangs into you!

PRESTINO: Unless the whole idea was the destruction of Giorgio Salvi!

ROCCA: Who can say?

DIEGO: But why should she do that? She had already got him to say he would marry her. She would hardly risk losing her fangs before she had got what she wanted.

ROCCA: Of course she had no idea how much was at stake!

DIEGO: Well, let's not call her a viper then. A viper has it all worked out. Maybe she would have bitten later, but not before the wedding. There's an absence of viperishness about the timing. Or, if it was done on purpose, it must have been with the intention of curing Salvi from the effects of the venom.

ROCCA: So you think . . .

DIEGO: Yes, I do, after what you have been saying. Your account of her behaviour just doesn't fit in with your accusations of scheming and betrayal. What schemer would first trick a man into marriage and then on the eve of the wedding tumble into bed with you!

ROCCA (*reacting violently*): Bed? Who said anything about bed? I never slept with her! Never! Do you think the thought ever even entered my head?

DIEGO (*astonished now, as are the others*): So you never . . . ?

THE OTHERS: You didn't? Well, then . . . ?

ROCCA: All I needed was evidence . . . which she'd have been ready enough to give! Just enough to convince him . . .

The door on the right opens and FRANCESCO SAVIO *enters, in a state of extreme agitation following his encounter with* DELIA MORELLO. *Her efforts to stop him fighting have evidently won him over, leaving him somewhat light-headed. He goes straight to* MICHELE ROCCA *and confronts him purposefully.*

FRANCESCO: What's all this? What the hell are you doing here? How dare you make such a commotion in my house?

ROCCA: I came to tell you . . .

FRANCESCO: There is nothing you can tell me!

ROCCA: Oh, yes, there is! I have a great deal to say to you, and not only to you . . .

FRANCESCO: I hope that is not supposed to be a threat . . .

ROCCA: Of course it's not a threat! I asked to speak to you . . .

FRANCESCO: You followed a lady here to my house . . .

ROCCA: I have just been explaining to your friends . . .

FRANCESCO: I am really not interested in your explanations. I suppose you don't deny that you followed this lady!

ROCCA: Yes, I followed her. Because if you are going to fight a duel with Signor Palegari . . .

FRANCESCO: A duel? I'm not going to fight a duel!

PRESTINO (*astonished*): What! What was that you said?

FRANCESCO: I've given up the idea. I am not fighting.

FIRST FRIEND, SECOND FRIEND, DIEGO (*together*): Have you gone mad? Are you serious? . . . You can't do that!

ROCCO (*with a sneer, speaking at the same time as the others, his words and sardonic laughter clearly audible*): You don't need to tell me! She has caught him! She has got him exactly where she wants him!

FRANCESCO (*angry, ready to resort to violence*): You shut your mouth! Or my God I'll . . .

PRESTINO (*getting between them and facing* FRANCESCO): Hold it, Francesco! Tell me first! You are not going to fight Palegari?

FRANCESCO: No. It is not right to go adding to her despair just to score some stupid little point of my own!

PRESTINO: You'll cause a bigger scandal if you don't fight! The conditions are drawn up, signed and sealed!

FRANCESCO: It would be ridiculous to fight with Palegari now!

PRESTINO: Ridiculous? Why?

FRANCESCO: Well, of course it would! It would be damn stupid! We're on the same side for heaven's sake! And come off it, Prestino, you know what I mean. Your trouble is you love duels and all the razzamatazz that goes with them.

PRESTINO: But you were the challenger! You challenged Palegari because he insulted you!

FRANCESCO: The whole thing is nonsensical! . . . as Diego said. So I suggest we drop it!

PRESTINO: I can't believe this!

ROCCA: It's her doing. She had made him promise not to touch her knight in shining armour!

FRANCESCO: Well, yes. And now that **you** are here . . .

ROCCA: Ah, so it's hands off Palegari and go for Rocca, is it?

FRANCESCO: Not at all! But here you are provoking me in my own house. What did you come for? What do you want of her?

PRESTINO: Drop it, Savio.

FRANCESCO: You have been following her around since yesterday evening!

PRESTINO: You can't fight **him**!

FRANCESCO: Nobody will be able to say I have changed for a less formidable opponent.

PRESTINO: You can't cancel! I'll go now, and tell Palegari that I am willing to fight him in your place . . .

FIRST FRIEND (*shouting at* FRANCESCO): You'll be disqualified!

PRESTINO: You'll be banned from duelling!

ROCCA: I can always overlook the disqualification!

FIRST FRIEND: You would have us to contend with! Because we are the ones who would disqualify him.

PRESTINO (*to* FRANCESCO): You simply wouldn't be able to find any seconds. Well, you've got the rest of the day to think about it. I'm going! I really can't stay here!

DIEGO: He'll think about it, all right! Lord, yes, he'll think think about it.

PRESTINO (*to the two friends*): I suggest we go. Coming? (*All three go out via the verandah and the garden.*)

DIEGO (*following them to the verandah and calling after them*): And might I recommend the maximum calm, gentlemen! No hasty decisions! (*Then, turning to* FRANCESCO.) And you had better watch your step as well!

FRANCESCO: Go to hell, Diego! (*Rounding on* ROCCA.) And you can get out! The door's over there! Let me know your terms: time, place, weapon, and I am at your disposal.

At this point DELIA MORELLO *appears in the doorway, right. As soon as she sees* MICHELE ROCCA, *so changed in appearance as to be almost unrecognisable, she knows that her defen-*

ces are useless. She is no longer able to hide behind the false front she has assumed as protection from the violent secret passion which has possessed them both from the moment they first set eyes on each other. All along they have tried to see their passion as concern and pity for Giorgio Salvi, each of them loudly protesting that their only interest has been in saving him. Stripped now of this lie, they stand pale and trembling face to face, each moved to sudden pity at the sight of the other. For a few moments they are speechless.

ROCCA (*his voice strangled by emotion*): Delia . . . Delia . . . (*He goes to embrace her.*)

DELIA (*sinking into his embrace*): No . . . no . . . Oh, my poor darling. (*To the horror and amazement of* DIEGO *and* FRANCESCO, *they continue to embrace with increasing frenzy.*)

ROCCA: Delia, oh my Delia!

DIEGO: Some hatred! Explains a lot, doesn't it? How about that? How about that, then?

FRANCESCO: It's outrageous! It's monstrous! How can they, with Salvi's death on their consciences!

ROCCA (*gripping her as he speaks, a beast of prey with its victim*): Monstrous, yes! But she must not leave me! She must stay with me and suffer with me!

DELIA (*appalled by the horror of it, fiercely struggling to free herself*): No! no! Get away from me! Get away! Let me go!

ROCCA (*still holding her*): No! This is where you belong! With me in my despair! In my arms!

DELIA: Let go! Let go of me, I say! . . . Murderer!

FRANCESCO: For God's sake, let her go! Let her go!

ROCCA (*to* FRANCESCO): You keep out of this!

DELIA (*freeing herself at last*): Don't you touch me! (FRANCESCO *and* DIEGO *manage to hold off* MICHELE ROCCA *who still wants to hurl himself at* DELIA.) I am not afraid of you! I'm really not! There is nothing you can do that will hurt me! You could kill me and it wouldn't hurt me!

ROCCA (*shouting above her words, still struggling to free himself from the clutches of* DIEGO *and* FRANCESCO): Delia!

Delia! I need to hold you close! I need . . . not to be alone!

DELIA (*still set on distancing herself*): I have no feelings at all. I thought I felt sorry for you, or afraid, or something. But I don't . . . I don't feel anything.

ROCCA (*desperate*): I'm going mad! Let me go, for God's sake!

DIEGO and FRANCESCO: They are raving! They're possessed! My God!

DELIA: Let him go! I'm not afraid of him! Yes! I let him kiss me! . . . quite coldly . . . not out of fear . . . not out of pity . . .

ROCCA: Oh, you devil! . . . I know, I know how cheap your kisses are . . . But I want you! I want you!

DELIA: I'd rather be dead! I'd rather you killed me! Anything would be preferable . . . another murder, or prison, or death. I want to go on suffering as I am suffering now.

ROCCA (*to* FRANCESCO *and* DIEGO *who are still restraining him*): I know she is worthless. Any value she has, she has from me, from the pain I have suffered on her account. I don't feel love! It is hatred I feel! Hatred!

DELIA: Hatred! Oh, yes, I feel hatred too!

ROCCA: I am awash with hatred, as if Salvi's spilt blood were flowing through my veins! (*He tears himself away from the grip of the two men.*) Help me, Delia! Help me! (*She runs away from him; he tries to catch her.*)

DELIA (*darting out of reach*): Oh, no! Oh no! Don't you dare come near me!

DIEGO and FRANCESCO (*again seizing* ROCCA): For God's sake, stop it, man! I'm warning you, Rocca!

DELIA: If he's playing for sympathy he's in for a nasty shock. I have no feeling either for him or for myself . . . And if **you** have any feelings for him, you'd better get him out of here quick.

ROCCA: How can you ask me to go? You know that my life ended with Salvi's death. I drowned in his blood.

DELIA: But wasn't it your idea to save your fiancée's brother from a dishonourable match?

ROCCA: That's damnable! You know that isn't true! Our stories are both lies, yours and mine!

DELIA: . . . both lies, yes, that's right! . . . both lies!

ROCCA: You wanted me, as I wanted you, right from the first moment!

DELIA: I wanted to punish you.

ROCCA: And I wanted to punish you. But when he died, your life ended too . . . in that pool of blood!

DELIA: Yes, it did! My life ended too! (*She runs to him like a flame, pushing aside* DIEGO *and* FRANCESCO *who are surprised into letting him go.*) . . . It's true! It's true!

ROCCA (*clasping her frantically in his arms*): All we can do now is cling together as the tide closes over our heads . . . like this! like this! I shan't be alone . . . and nor will you . . . We shall be together . . . like this! . . . like this!

DIEGO: If it lasts!

ROCCA (*as he carries her off down the steps into the garden, leaving* DIEGO *and* FRANCESCO *dumbfounded and appalled*): Come, my love, come with me! Let me take you away!

FRANCESCO: They must be out of their minds!

DIEGO: What about you, my old friend? You can't see yourself!

CURTAIN

SECOND CHORAL INTERLUDE

Once again the curtain rises as soon as it has been lowered, revealing the same section of the passage encircling the auditorium that we saw in the first interlude. There is a small door at the end of the passage leading to the 'stage'. This time the audience is slow to emerge. The front-of-house staff, uniformed attendants, programme-sellers and so on, seem apprehensive. They have seen MORENO *escape the clutches of her three friends at the end of the Act and rush down the passage and out onto the stage. A deafening din of shouting and clapping is heard coming from the auditorium. The audience is growing wilder by the minute, either because they are impatient for the cast to take their curtain-call, or because they can hear mysterious cries and peculiar noises coming from beyond the lowered curtain. These voices of course can be heard more distinctly out here in the passage.*

UNIFORMED ATTENDANT (MALE): What the devil's going on?

SECOND UNIFORMED ATTENDANT (MALE): It's a Pirandello first night. Usual hullabaloo!

PROGRAMME SELLER (FEMALE): Listen! They are applauding but the cast aren't taking their bow!

ATTENDANT (FEMALE): But the shouting is coming from the stage! Can you hear it?

SECOND ATTENDANT (MALE): **And** there's a hell of a row coming from out in front!

SECOND ATTENDANT (FEMALE): Do you think it's to do with that lady who just rushed past?

FIRST ATTENDANT (MALE): More than likely. She was right out of control. They had an impossible job holding her.

FIRST ATTENDANT (FEMALE): She ran onto the stage!

FIRST ATTENDANT (MALE): She was trying to get on at the end of the First Act as well.

THIRD ATTENDANT (FEMALE): They're shouting blue murder! Listen!

Two or three of the doors to the boxes now open, and some members of the audience come out looking very perturbed. The uproar swells whenever a door is opened.

PEOPLE FROM THE BOXES (*as they emerge*): Something's going on on the stage!
But whatever's happening? Is it a fight?
They are yelling their heads off:
There hasn't been a curtain-call or anything!

More members of the audience appear, looking even more dismayed than the last lot. They eye the small door leading onto the 'stage'. Almost immediately dozens more rush in from the left. All are exclaiming 'Whatever's up? What's happening? What is it?' *Still more come flocking in from the stalls. There is general consternation and dismay.*

CONFUSED VOICES: They are fighting on the stage!
                     Can you hear it? There!
                     On the stage?
                     Why? Why?
                     God knows!
                     Excuse me, may I get by?
                     What has happened?
                     Whatever next?
                     What the hell's going on?
                     May I pass, Please?
                     Has the play finished?
                     What about the Third Act?
                     Excuse me, please, may I get by?
                     Fine. Four o'clock tomorrow! See you!
                     Just listen to that racket on the stage!
                     I'm going to get my coat!
                     Hey! Did you hear that?
                     It's disgraceful!
                     It's disgusting!
                     It's a devil of a row! What's it about?
                     Well . . . they **say** . . .
                     Nobody seems to know . . .
                     What the hell!? . . .
                     Look! Look! Over there!
                     Someone's opened the door!

The door from the stage is opened and from beyond it we are momentarily able to hear the confused cries of actors, actresses, the DIRECTOR, MORENO *and her three friends. These sounds form a kind of counterpoint to the chorus of voices provided by members of the 'audience' on the real stage who now crowd round the door, to angry protestations from various exasperated individuals who want to break through the throng and make their escape.*

ACTORS' VOICES FROM THE 'STAGE': Get out! Go away!
Get her out of here! God, you've a cheek! The woman's a
pest! How dare you . . . ! My God, you'll pay for this! Get
the hell out, go on!

MORENO's VOICE: . . . but it's criminal!

DIRECTOR's VOICE: I must ask you to leave!

FRIEND's VOICE: She's only a girl for heaven's sake!

MORENO's VOICE: . . . I suddenly saw red!

FRIEND's VOICE: . . . Consider her feelings! Poor **lady**!

ACTORS' VOICES: Some lady! . . . She means trouble! . . .
Get rid of her! Get her out! . . .

ACTRESSES' VOICES: . . . Evil bitch! . . . Hard-faced cow!

ACTORS' VOICES: My God! She can thank her stars she's
female . . . She has bloody asked for it, hasn't she! . . . Get
her out!

DIRECTOR's VOICE: Clear the stage for Christ's sake!

VOICES FROM AMONG THE 'AUDIENCE' (*on this side of
the door, all speaking at once against a background of
booing, hissing and applause*): Moreno! Moreno! Who's
Moreno? Someone has struck the leading lady! Who has
struck the leading lady? Moreno! Moreno! Who's Moreno?
The leading lady? No, someone has walloped Pirandello!
Walloped Pirandello? Who would do that? Who? Who?
Moreno! No, the leading lady! Pirandello has biffed the leading lady? No! You've got it all wrong! The leading lady went
for Pirandello! No! That wasn't it! It was Moreno! She
slapped the actress in the face!

VOICES FROM THE 'STAGE': Quiet, now! Order! Clear
the stage! Out of the way, you hooligans! And you, Missis,
aren't you ashamed? Out! Out! Make way! Gangway,
please!

VOICES FROM AMONG THE 'AUDIENCE': Get them out!
Get those hooligans out! Quiet, now! Sh . . . sh . . . sh . . . Was
that really Signorina Moreno? Shshsh! . . . go on, out! Let's
get on with the play! Get rid of those nuisances! Down with
Pirandello! Up with Pirandello! It's all Pirandello's fault!
Come on, that's enough! Make a gangway! Gangway please!
Make way!

The crowd of spectators divides to let through a bunch of actors and actresses who are walking out in protest. They are followed by the company's ADMINISTRATIVE DIRECTOR *and by the* THEATRE MANAGER *who want them to go on with the play. In the heat of the ensuing confusion the assembled 'audience' members soon tire of listening quietly and hasten to break in with their own vociferous commentary.*

THEATRE MANAGER: For Christ's sake, have some sense! Do you want us to have to close?

ACTORS AND ACTRESSES (*all at once*): We're not taking this! . . . I'm going! . . . We're all going! . . . It's really not on! . . . It's bloody disgraceful! . . . We're walking out in protest! . . . It's a protest!

ADMINISTRATIVE DIRECTOR: What do you mean, protest? Who are you protesting against?

ONE OF THE ACTORS: Against Pirandello! How dare he do this!

ANOTHER ACTOR: And the Director! He should never have put it on!

THEATRE MANAGER: But actors can't just walk out even in protest! You can't just down tools and leave a play half-way through! It's anarchy!

VOICES FROM AMONG THE 'AUDIENCE' (*backing the actors*): That's the stuff! You tell him! . . . Who are they? . . . They're the actors, don't you see? . . . No, I don't see . . . But they are right! They are right! They **should** protest!

ACTORS (*to the* THEATRE MANAGER, *speaking above the hubbub*): Oh, yes, we can! That's just what we can do!

CHARACTER ACTOR: It's this business of the *comédie à clef*?

VOICES OF NAÏVE 'AUDIENCE' MEMBERS: What's a *comédie à clef*? A comedy with a key? What sort of key? What does he mean, a comedy with a key?

ACTORS (*as before to* THEATRE MANAGER *and* DIRECTOR): We are going and you can't stop us!

VOICES OF 'AUDIENCE' MEMBERS IN THE KNOW: Well, it's no secret! It all came out! . . . There was a fearful scandal! . . . Everyone knows now . . . the Moreno case . . . And she's here, in this theatre!... she went barging onto the stage ... and struck the leading lady* across the face!

OTHER 'AUDIENCE' MEMBERS (*including Pirandello supporters and others to whom this information is news, speaking together and in some confusion*): Well, you couldn't tell! Nobody realised!... We were enjoying it... We want the Third Act... We've paid for our seats ... Come on, we like it!... It's good!... Give us the Third Act!

ONE OF THE ACTORS: Yes, but look, we're professional people! We can't be pushed around!

ANOTHER ACTOR: Let's go! I'm going, anyway!

CHARACTER ACTRESS: The leading lady's* gone, so why not!

VOICES FROM AMONG THE 'AUDIENCE': Has she left the theatre?... Why?... Which way did she go?... Did she go by the stage door?

CHARACTER ACTRESS: She was assaulted on the stage by a woman from the audience!

ARGUMENTATIVE VOICES FROM THE 'AUDIENCE': She was assaulted?... Yes, the Moreno woman gave her a slap in the face!... Quite right, too!... Who was it?... Who did it?... Moreno... Why?... What did she do that for?... The leading lady?*

ONE OF THE ACTORS: Because she recognised herself as Delia in the play!

ANOTHER ACTOR: She thought it was a plot! She thought we were all of us trying to create a scandal!

CHARACTER ACTRESS (*to 'audience' members*): Hard work has gone into this play! It seems a funny way to show appreciation!

BARON NUTI (*still restrained by his two friends, trembling with uncontrollable emotion, making his way towards centre stage*): You are right! It's an outrageous insult! You have every right to walk out!

ONE OF HIS FRIENDS: Don't get involved! Come on, come on, let's go!

---

* *Translator's Note:* the name of the actress playing the part of Delia Morello could be substituted here if wished.

BARON NUTI: It's a viciously cruel thing to do! You have held two people up to public ridicule, two people who inwardly are still weeping tears of blood.

THEATRE MANAGER (*at the end of his tether*): So the performance is taking place out here, now is it!

HOSTILE VOICES FROM AMONG THE 'AUDIENCE': Nuti's right! . . . It's outrageous! It shouldn't be allowed! . . . Stop the play! Walk out! . . . It's defamation of character!

FAVOURABLE VOICES: That's ridiculous! . . . Honestly, some people! . . . I just don't see it . . . Where's the slander? . . . Defamation of character? . . . Rubbish!

THEATRE MANAGER: Is this a theatre or a madhouse?

BARON NUTI (*seizing one of the 'favourable' speakers by the lapels amid the general stunned silence inspired by his fury and wild looks*): So you think it's all right, do you? All right to take a living person like me, and to stick me up there on a stage for all to see, to make an Aunt Sally of my agonizing pain? To make me say words I have never spoken? . . . to do things I should never in my life have dreamed of doing?

During the silence which follows these words the small door from the stage opens and LA MORENO *is dragged out, dishevelled, crying, almost fainting, by her three escorts. The* PRODUCER's *words to her which follow will ring out like a reply to what* NUTI *has just said. As he speaks, the crowd turns towards them, making way for them.* BARON NUTI *lets go of the man he has gripped by the coat and turns too, muttering 'What's happening?'*

PRODUCER: Well, you have seen for yourself! Neither the Author nor the actress have ever set eyes on you before!

LA MORENO: But she said what I said! She did what I did! Exactly what I did! It was me! I was watching myself!

PRODUCER: You must have wanted to think it was you!

LA MORENO: No, no! That's not true . . . The horror! . . . The sheer horror of seeing myself in that last act! You know what you did? You made me kiss him! How could you make me kiss him? (*She suddenly comes almost face to face with* NUTI

and shrieks, covering her face with her hands.) Oh my God!
It's him! It's him!
BARON NUTI: Amelia! Amelia!

*The 'audience' members are visibly shaken, hardly believing
their eyes as they see reappearing live before them, the characters and situation from the preceding act of the play. Their
astonishment is conveyed by the expressions on their faces, and
in hasty whispers and the odd exclamation.*

VOICES FROM AMONG THE 'AUDIENCE': Look! . . .
There they are! . . . Oh! Oh! . . . Both of them! . . . It's the
same scene! . . . Look! Look!
LA MORENO (*desperately to her companions*): Get him away
from me! I don't want to see him!
HER COMPANIONS: Yes, come on, let's go!
BARON NUTI (*flinging himself upon her*): No! No! You must
come with me! You must come with me!
LA MORENO (*struggling in his grasp*): Let me go! Let me go!
Murderer!
BARON NUTI: You got that from the play!
LA MORENO: Let me go! I'm not afraid of you!
BARON NUTI: But they told the truth! That's what we've got to
do! . . . be punished together! Didn't you hear them say so?
Everybody knows about it now! Come with me! Come with me!
LA MORENO: No! Let me go! I hate you! I hate you, you
bastard!
BARON NUTI: It was true, too, about us drowning in La Vela's
blood. We both died then. You must, must come with me!
(*And he drags her away, disappearing offstage left, followed
by a large gaggle of the spectators who comment loudly.*)
MEMBERS OF CROWD OFFSTAGE: Look at that! . . . Would
you believe it . . . It's incredible! . . . It's extraordinary! . . . Just
look at them! . . . Well, I mean, it's Delia Morello and Michele
Rocca! (*A number of spectators remain on stage, watching them
leave, and commenting in much the same way.*)
STUPID SPECTATOR: They hated the play, and then they go
and do exactly the same thing!

PRODUCER: I know! And she had the nerve to come on stage and physically attack my leading actress. 'How could you make me kiss him!' she said.

OTHERS: It's unbelievable! . . . unbelievable!

INTELLIGENT SPECTATOR: On the contrary, it's absolutely natural! They saw a mirror-image of themselves and they rebelled against it . . . They were particularly horrified by that final clinch!

PRODUCER: But then they went and did exactly the same thing themselves!

INTELLIGENT SPECTATOR: Of course they did! That's right! They couldn't help themselves! Here, in front of our very eyes they went and did exactly what art predicted they would do! (*This gets a favourable reception from the group of spectators, some of whom clap or laugh.*)

THE ACTOR WHO PLAYS DIEGO CINCI (*moving forward from the direction of the stage door*): Don't be too sure! Those two, eh? Well, listen. I am the actor who plays Diego Cinci in the production, and Diego, I think has got it right. As soon as those two get through that door, they . . . (*He breaks off.*) The fact is you haven't seen the Third Act.

'AUDIENCE' MEMBERS: You are right! We haven't seen the Third Act! What happens? What happens? Tell us what happens next!

ACTOR PLAYING DIEGO CINCI: All sorts of things happen, all sorts of things . . . and even after the end of the Third Act, well . . . other things . . . other things . . . (*Still speaking, he leaves.*)

THEATRE MANAGER (*to PRODUCER*): Not expecting to hold a public assembly here, are you, sir?

PRODUCER: What do you expect **me** to do? Have the place cleared?

ADMINISTRATIVE DIRECTOR OF THE COMPANY: We can't give you a Third Act anyway. The actors have gone home!

PRODUCER: I don't know what you're asking me to do about it! Have a notice put up or something. Tell them just to go.

THEATRE MANAGER: There are still people in the House.

PRODUCER: Fine! I'll deal with those. I'll step in front of the curtain and get rid of them.

THEATRE MANAGER: Yes, yes, do that, please! (*While the PRODUCER makes his way towards the small door to the stage, the THEATRE MANAGER starts shooing people off.*) The show is over now, ladies and gentlemen. The theatre is closing. Sorry! We're closing now.

The Curtain falls, and as soon as it has fallen the PRODUCER steps in front of the footlights and addresses the real audience.

PRODUCER: Ladies and Gentlemen, I am sorry to have to announce that owing to certain unfortunate incidents—which took place this evening at the end of Act Two, Act Three cannot now be performed.

THE END

GRAFTED

L'Innesto

1917

*English version by
Robert Rietty*

CHARACTERS

GIORGIO BANTI
LAURA, his wife
GIULIETTA, Laura's sister
SIGNORA FRANCESCA BETTI, their mother
ARTURO NELLI, a lawyer and friend of the family
SIGNORA NELLI, his wife
DOCTOR ROMERI
MARIA, Laura's maid
MANFREDI, a manservant in the Banti's home
ZENA, a peasant
FILIPPO, an old gardener

Translator's Note: The date when this play was written has to be borne well in mind—1918. The war had just ended and Europe was in turmoil. Moral values were being questioned, conventions thrown to the wind, a revolution was occurring in the minds of Italians who had accepted their parents' and predecessors' conduct. In Italian society a young lady could still not go out with a man unless accompanied by a chaperon. If she did, for the sake of propriety, she had to describe him or introduce him as her 'fiancé'. It mattered little if she changed her fiancé regularly—'Society' was satisfied that all was 'above board' if she was (for the time being at least) 'engaged' to her male companion.

ACT I

The BANTI's *tastefully furnished drawing-room in Rome. The main door into the room is at the back, centre, and there are doors to the right and to the left. It is afternoon in the late summer.*

When the curtain rises SIGNORA NELLI, *paying a call on the* BANTI's, *is standing by an occasional table, glancing at an illustrated magazine. After a few moments* SIGNORA FRANCESCA BETTI *enters left with her daughter* GIULIETTA. *They are dressed ready to go out.*

SIGNORA FRANCESCA BETTI *is elderly, provincial, wealthy. The sort of person who wears dresses which are rather too tight and too fashionable, contrasting with her somewhat uncultured appearance and way of talking.*

GIULIETTA, *her daughter is young, blasé, affecting a superior attitude, especially towards her mother.*

SIGNORA NELLI *is a fashionable sort of woman, beginning to go to seed, who still tries to maintain her position in a milieu to which she no longer really belongs.*

MARIA (*approaching*): Would you care to wait in here, Signora Nelli. The Signora hasn't come home yet; but her mother and sister are here, waiting for her. I'll tell them that you've come.

SIGNORA NELLI: Thank you, Maria. (*A moment's pause. A clock strikes the half hour.* SIGNORA BETTI *and* GIULIETTA *enter.*)

SIGNORA BETTI: My dear Signora Nelli . . . how nice to see you.

SIGNORA NELLI: How are you, Francesca? Oh, Giulietta; are you well?

GIULIETTA: Fine thank you, and you?

SIGNORA NELLI: Yes thank you.

SIGNORA BETTI: Well, as you see, here we are, waiting—like you.

SIGNORA NELLI: Yes—the maid told me.

SIGNORA BETTI: We've been waiting for about an hour! No, what am I saying—it must be more than that—two at least!

GIULIETTA: It really is odd, you know. I'm quite worried.

SIGNORA NELLI: Why? Has she been out so long?

GIULIETTA: Since six o'clock this morning. Just think of that!

SIGNORA NELLI: Really? Did Laura leave the house at six?

SIGNORA BETTI (*resentfully*): Now, Giulietta, if you go saying 'six o'clock' like that, goodness knows what ideas you'll put into people's heads. You ought to explain that she took her . . . her . . . what d'you call it?

GIULIETTA (*softly, bored*): Paintbox.

SIGNORA BETTI: That's it . . . her paintbox—with her.

SIGNORA NELLI: Oh! Splendid! Has Laura taken up painting again, then?

SIGNORA BETTI: Yes, three days ago. She goes out into the country, to the woods, I believe.

GIULIETTA: Woods, Mother?! To the Villa Giulia gardens!

SIGNORA BETTI: Oh, yes, of course. I've always lived in Naples, and I don't know much about these parks here in Rome, I'm afraid.

GIULIETTA: All right, Mother! But you know, Signora Nelli, yesterday and the day before she was back by eleven at the latest. Now, it's getting on for three, and . . .

SIGNORA NELLI: I expect she wanted to finish her sketch.

SIGNORA BETTI: Of course, that must be it! Don't you think so, Giulietta?

GIULIETTA: Well . . .

SIGNORA NELLI: If she went out with her paintbox there's no need to worry. That explains it.

GIULIETTA: Oh, no! That would **not** explain it, I'm afraid. When an artist goes out three days running at dawn, it shows that she wants to catch certain early morning light effects that can't be seen later in the day.

SIGNORA NELLI: Oh, is Giulietta a painter, too?

GIULIETTA: Good Heavens, no!

SIGNORA BETTI: Don't you believe her! She knows quite a lot about it. As much as Laura. What a wonderful thing education is, Signora Nelli! I've always loved it. I wasn't able to have any myself, but my daughters, thank goodness, had the best teachers . . . French, English . . . Music . . . and Laura, who had a flair for it; we had **her** taught painting, too, by Professor Dalbuono—you know him, of course—everybody's heard of him. Giulietta wouldn't study it, but then, of course . . .

SIGNORA NELLI: . . . Being with her sister, I suppose . . .

SIGNORA BETTI: . . . Yes, she picked up quite a bit.

GIULIETTA (*turning away—impatiently*): Oh, Mother!

SIGNORA BETTI: What's the matter now, Giulietta?

GIULIETTA: Oh, nothing! Nothing!

SIGNORA NELLI (*pretending not to understand the girl's embarrassment on account of her mother's silly chatter*): Come, Giulietta, don't worry like this! There's some sense in what you say, but don't you think Laura might suddenly have taken it into her head to start some other sketch?

GIULIETTA (*coldly, agreeing out of politeness*): Quite likely, yes.

SIGNORA NELLI: If she has started painting again with her old enthusiasm . . .

GIULIETTA: Oh no! It's not Laura who's so keen on it. In fact I don't think she really cares for it any longer.

SIGNORA NELLI: What do you mean?

SIGNORA BETTI: Well, when you get married, you know, these things are . . . what d'you call them? . . . accomplishments, that's it, just accomplishments, for a girl. Don't you think so? However, my son-in law likes them. To tell the truth, he encourages her.

SIGNORA NELLI: And so he should! It would really be a shame for Laura to give it up when she's so talented.

GIULIETTA: That's not why my brother-in-law does it! Perhaps if Laura thought her husband were **really** interested in her art . . . but she knows that he encourages her to take up her palette again, just as he would encourage her to take up . . . well, any other hobby.

SIGNORA BETTI: Do you think that's a bad thing? You must have something to do in your spare time when you're grown-up, like my two girls, eh, Signora Nelli? But . . . do you know what's the real trouble in this house? They haven't any children!

SIGNORA NELLI: Don't mention children to me! If you knew how I envy Laura! She married two years before me, didn't she? That'll be seven years ago. And in five years I've had three.

SIGNORA BETTI: Ah, yes, but—if I may say so—it's obvious you put your heart and soul into the business!

SIGNORA NELLI (*laughing—pretending to be shocked*): Oh! No! Really! They just came . . .

SIGNORA BETTI: Just one, I say . . . they ought to have at least one.

SIGNORA NELLI: I always thought Laura and her husband got on so well together.

SIGNORA BETTI: Oh, they do. (*In a soft confidential tone.*) Too well, in fact, Signora Nelli! Too well.

SIGNORA NELLI (*also quietly, rather at a loss, but smiling a little*): Too well? What do you mean?

SIGNORA BETTI: I mean that . . . well, you know how it is, in the early days of married life, when husband and wife are both young and very much in love, whenever the question of children crops up, the husband . . . (*She searches for the word.*) 'Bridles'—d'you know what I mean? He fights shy, because he's afraid he won't be able to keep his little wife all to himself any longer.

SIGNORA NELLI: Oh, I know! But then a year or two go by, perhaps three . . . and . . . Does Giorgio now want a child?

SIGNORA BETTI: No, it's Laura who does. She wants one so badly. Giorgio **says** he wants one, just for her sake.

GIULIETTA: And, of course, Laura wants one for her own sake.

SIGNORA BETTI: What do you mean? Why do you talk like that? Do you want Signora Nelli to think that Laura isn't happy with her husband?

GIULIETTA: No, no, Mother! I didn't say that. But when you consider that they've been married, not merely three years, but seven . . . !

SIGNORA BETTI: You don't understand! Signora Nelli, you know what happens to a wife after so many years if they have no children? She wastes away, I tell you! So does the husband. They both waste away—it's only natural. I don't like to speak in front of Giulietta, but it's just the opposite of what she imagines. Because in time the husband loses his fear that if his wife becomes a mother, she may cease to be a good wife, and . . . and . . . well, **you** see what I'm driving at, don't you?

SIGNORA NELLI: Oh, yes. I understand.

SIGNORA BETTI: These blessed girls! Goodness knows what dreams they have about life!

GIULIETTA: Really, Mother! You know I never dream!

SIGNORA BETTI: Oh, no, miss! You don't dream. And I suppose you think it's a fine thing not to dream? I can't stand these modern girls, Signora Nelli, with all their airs and graces, pretending to be so . . . so . . .

SIGNORA NELLI (*suggesting, with a smile*): *Fanée.*

SIGNORA BETTI: What did you say?

SIGNORA NELLI: *Fanée.*

SIGNORA BETTI (*not knowing the word at all*): . . . Yes, that's it.

GIULIETTA (*contemptuously*): It's the fashion, Mother.

SIGNORA BETTI: I don't know any French, but I do know that I don't like that fashion one little bit!

MARIA (*calling off. She is very agitated*): Signora! Signora! (*The* MAID *enters.*) It's Signora Laura. Come quick!

SIGNORA BETTI: My daughter?

SIGNORA NELLI: Heavens! What's happened?

MARIA: Manfredi and a Police Officer are bringing her up. She's been hurt.

SIGNORA BETTI: What? Laura hurt?

GIULIETTA (*with a cry, running to the door*): I knew it! (*Voices are heard off.*)

MANFREDI: Just one more step, Signora. Keep your arm round my shoulder.

POLICE OFFICER: Careful now . . . slowly. (LAURA *enters, supported by the* POLICE OFFICER *and* MANFREDI.)

SIGNORA BETTI: Oh, Laura! What have they done to you, my poor child?

LAURA (*falling on her mother's neck, a prey to a growing convulsion of shuddering despair*): Mother! Mother! Mother!

SIGNORA BETTI: Where have you been hurt? Show me where.

GIULIETTA: Her mouth is bleeding—and her neck's all scratched! Can't you see?

SIGNORA NELLI: Oh, my God! It looks like a wound!

SIGNORA BETTI: Laura, my darling . . .

SIGNORA NELLI: How did it happen? Who did it?

GIULIETTA: Here, Mother—let her sit down. Don't you see she can't stand?

SIGNORA BETTI: Oh yes, sit down, child, sit down. But who would want to attack you? Who was it?

GIULIETTA: Who was it, Manfredi?

MANFREDI: I don't know, Signorina. Perhaps the Police Officer here . . .

GIULIETTA: Yes, you tell us, Officer—who was it?

OFFICER (*embarrassed*): Well . . . the lady has been . . . assaulted.

SIGNORA NELLI (*a stifled cry*): Oh!

GIULIETTA (*kneeling and trying to take her sister in her arms*): Oh, Laura! Tell me, tell me . . . what has he done to you?

LAURA (*instinctively, but with anxious affection, pushing her sister away*): No, no! Not you, Giulietta—I can't tell you. Go away. Please go . . .

GIULIETTA (*sitting back on her heels, bewildered*): Why?

SIGNORA BETTI (*guessing the nature of the assault on her daughter. Quietly*): Oh, not that! Good God—not that! Signora Nelli. Please . . . please take Giulietta away.

SIGNORA NELLI: Come along, dear. Come with me.

GIULIETTA (*tearfully*): But, why?

SIGNORA NELLI (*going*): It's best to leave your sister alone for a while . . . she needs rest and . . . (GIULIETTA *glances at the* POLICE OFFICER *realises she must go, and starts to sob as* SIGNORA NELLI *takes her out of the room through the centre door.*)

SIGNORA BETTI: What did he do, my child?

LAURA: Look Mother . . . my neck! Look!

SIGNORA BETTI: But, who did it? Who?

LAURA (*unable to speak through her sobs. Three times, between the frightening shudder of her whole body, she bursts out*): A brute! A brute! A brute! (*Then a deep sigh.*)

SIGNORA BETTI: Oh, my God—she's fainted. Here, Maria, help me take her into the bedroom.

MARIA: Yes, Signora.

MANFREDI: Let me help you, Signora.

SIGNORA BETTI (*going*): No, Manfredi— we can manage. Go and 'phone for the doctor—quick!—Doctor Romeri.

MANFREDI: I have already rung his home, Signora.

SIGNORA BETTI: Good. Come, my darling. (SIGNORA BETTI, LAURA *and the maid exit left to the bedroom.*)

MANFREDI (*after a moment*): Have they caught the man, Officer?

POLICE OFFICER: Not yet, as far as I know.

MANFREDI: Where did it happen?

ROMERI (*off—approaching*): That's all right, I know where to go.

MANFREDI: Ah, here's the Doctor. (DOCTOR ROMERI *enters centre in haste.*)

ROMERI: Where is she?

MANFREDI: In the signora's bedroom, Doctor. This way.

ROMERI: Thank you. (*At this moment the voices of* GIORGIO BANTI, ARTURO NELLI *and* SIGNORA NELLI *are heard, off.*)

SIGNORA NELLI: Yes, the doctor's just gone in.

GIORGIO (*calling off stage*): Doctor! Doctor!

MANFREDI (*knocking at the bedroom door, calling through the door*): The doctor's here, Signora.

GIORGIO (*enters centre*): Doctor—is she hurt?

ROMERI: I don't know. I've only just arrived. (*The bedroom door opens.*)

SIGNORA BETTI: Oh Doctor—thank Heaven you've come. You too, Giorgio.

GIORGIO (*calling as he runs into the bedroom*): Laura ... Laura, darling ... (*The door closes.*)

MANFREDI: Please call me if you require anything, Signora Nelli.

SIGNORA NELLI: Yes, yes, of course, Manfredi.

NELLI: Let's hope it's not serious, my dear.

SIGNORA NELLI: You should have seen her when they brought her in. She was in a dreadful state, poor thing.

NELLI: Tell me, Officer ... was it ... was it an assault?

POLICE OFFICER: Yes. Rape, I'm afraid, sir. At Villa Giulia, apparently.

SIGNORA NELLI: She had gone there to sketch.

POLICE OFFICER: I don't know much about it yet. I've just been put in charge of the preliminary investigations.

SIGNORA NELLI: She's been going there every day for the last three days.

NELLI: Always to the same spot?

SIGNORA NELLI: So it seems. Giulietta says so. She went every morning at six.

NELLI: What, alone?!

POLICE OFFICER: A keeper at the Villa found her lying on the ground.

SIGNORA NELLI: Unconscious?

POLICE OFFICER: He says there were no signs of life. Apparently he had heard her shout just before.

SIGNORA NELLI: Then why didn't he run to help her?

POLICE OFFICER: He says it was too far. The Villa's always deserted.

NELLI: What madness to go there alone like that!

SIGNORA NELLI: Look, Arturo, here's her paintbox.

POLICE OFFICER: Yes, and her hat ... (*A moment's pause, filled with the apprehension that one feels when faced with an object that has been the witness of a recent drama.*) They were found by the keeper a long way from the place where the lady was lying. Evidently she had tried to run away ...

NELLI: ... And was followed?

POLICE OFFICER: I don't know. She was found lying on her face—in a hedge of brambles.

SIGNORA NELLI (*shuddering in horror*): Oh! Perhaps she was trying to jump over ... poor soul!

POLICE OFFICER: Perhaps—and, being over-taken just there ... (*He hesitates.*)

SIGNORA NELLI: She was all torn and scratched! Her neck and mouth ... Oh, it's pitiful!

NELLI (*shaking his head with bitter derision*): Among the thorns!

POLICE OFFICER: He was a powerfully built man. The keeper saw him.

NELLI (*anxiously*): Oh, did he?

POLICE OFFICER: Yes—running away from the hedge. Quite a young man, too.

NELLI: If the keeper saw him, why didn't he chase him?

POLICE OFFICER: All he could think of was helping the lady, and ... (*He breaks off as the bedroom door opens and excited voices are heard, off.*)

ROMERI (*off*): No, no, I tell you! I'm sorry, but I must ask you to ...

SIGNORA BETTI (*off*): Please, Giorgio! Please! (GIORGIO *enters, clearly distressed. The others remain in the doorway.*)

GIORGIO: But I have every right to be told! I must know!

ROMERI: Of course you'll be told—but later. It's most important that your wife should have rest now.

GIORGIO: But I want to ...

ROMERI: I tell you for the present you must not question her—or even let her see you! Please, Signor Nelli—keep him in here!

NELLI (*sympathetically*): Come, come, Giorgio.

GIORGIO: But I ... (*He stops, breathing with difficulty as though he were trying to stifle a sob.*)

SIGNORA BETTI: Signora Nelli, would you be kind enough to take Giulietta home for me?

SIGNORA NELLI: Yes, of course. Shall we go now?

SIGNORA BETTI: Yes, please. Tell her I'm staying here ... as long as I can. Good gracious! It's getting late—I shall have to go and see to my poor husband—you know how ill he is.

SIGNORA NELLI: Yes, I know. If I can do anything . . . ?

SIGNORA BETTI: No, no, thank you all the same. He won't let anybody else touch him. Ah, there's Giulietta. (GIULIETTA *appears at the centre door.*) Giulietta dear, you're going home with Signora Nelli. I'll come just as soon as I can.

GIULIETTA: What about Laura? Where is she?

SIGNORA BETTI: In her bedroom.

GIULIETTA: Can't I even see her?

SIGNORA BETTI: No, no. She must be left alone for the present. Go along now, go home to your poor father—and don't say a word to him, mind!

GIULIETTA: But . . . what is it, Mother? What's wrong?

SIGNORA BETTI: It's nothing, nothing! Take her away, Signora Nelli.

SIGNORA NELLI: Yes. Come along, Giulietta.

GIULIETTA (*resolutely*): Giorgio, do **you** say it's nothing?

GIORGIO: I?

GIULIETTA: I want to hear **you** say it.

GIORGIO: I . . . what can I tell you? I don't know! I don't know!

SIGNORA BETTI: Go along, there's a good girl. You keep me standing here when . . . (*Going.*) Go home with Signora Nelli. (*She goes into the bedroom closing the door.*)

SIGNORA NELLI: Come, Giulietta dear. Come along. (*As they go out centre.*) The doctor's in there with her at the moment, and it's much better if she hasn't too many people around her . . .

GIORGIO: Officer what do you know about this? Tell me! That . . . fiend must be caught and handed over to me at once; handed over to me, I tell you. Because, for a crime like this, if the law gets hold of him, he'll only get . . . How much is it, Nelli?—You're a lawyer—two or three years' imprisonment, isn't it? But I have the right to kill him! Do you understand?

POLICE OFFICER: I don't know anything about that, sir. I'm here only to investigate.

NELLI: But what's the use when there's nothing to find out?

GIORGIO: What do you mean?

NELLI: Nothing to find out, no basis for an investigation! Good Lord, surely things have gone far enough.

GIORGIO: I don't understand you.

NELLI: The matter has gone far enough as it is, I tell you. Your wife has been assaulted in a public park, and the thief . . .

GIORGIO: Thief, you call him?

NELLI: Yes, the thief—some wretch or other—has got away and unfortunately can't be traced. That's where the matter **has** to end. What more can be done?

GIORGIO: Oh, no, Nelli—you're making a mistake there!

POLICE OFFICER: I have my orders. This is a criminal offence and . . .

NELLI: . . . And that means that I shall go to the Police Court or call on the Commissioner myself. You may go, Officer, do you hear?

GIORGIO: And what about me? It's all very well for the others to leave it at that, but what about me?

NELLI: You? What do you think you can do? Do you really imagine that if the police catch him they'll hand him over to you, and let you kill him? Of course they won't! They'll let the law take its course. It's true that—as you say—for a crime like this (for which, had you been there at the time, you could have killed the man in defence of your wife without incurring any penalty yourself), for a crime like this the law gives no more than two or three years imprisonment. Do you want that to happen? Think of the publicity—the reports in the newspapers. Come, come! All right, Officer, you may go now.

POLICE OFFICER (*still not very sure*): Well, seeing that the doctor says she's not to be questioned for the time being, I . . . I suppose I can go.

NELLI: Yes, yes. Don't you worry—I'll come and see the Commissioner myself.

POLICE OFFICER (*going*): Good-day then, gentlemen. I hope the signora will be all right.

NELLI: Good-day, Officer. (*The OFFICER exits centre.*) It's always the same! When they're needed, these people are never there: then they insist on shoving in their noses when it's too late; and only make matters worse. Giorgio, think what effect it might have on your poor wife right now if the press gets hold of the story. You don't want people thinking . . .

GIORGIO: What's the good of talking to me about other people! What difference does it make to me what they think?

NELLI: That's how you feel today, I know. But you'll see tomorrow that it does make a difference.

GIORGIO: In the first place, it's no good trying to avoid publicity, because everybody knows already, both here and where she was found. But even if no one else knew, **I** know; (*quietly*) and don't you see that for me everything is finished now!

NELLI: Yes, Giorgio, I do see, and I can understand the horror you are feeling at this moment. But you must overcome it. (*As* GIORGIO *is about to say something.*) Yes, you must overcome it by the pity . . . the sympathy you are bound to have for your poor wife.

GIORGIO: Sympathy? Don't talk to me about sympathy!

NELLI: Have you none to give her?

GIORGIO: How little does that word convey! What sort of sympathy do you expect me to have? The same sort as all of you, and anybody who hears about this outrage? Oh, that's easy—nobody can refuse her that! But, I'm her husband! I'm the only one who can feel the full horror of this outrage— which has been done, not only to her, but to me, too!

NELLI: Yes, Giorgio, don't imagine I don't understand how you feel, but . . .

GIORGIO (*quietly, almost to himself*): Nobody but I can know the **real** torment I feel—not even she.

NELLI: I know, Giorgio, I know. It is cruel indeed. But what do you propose to do?

GIORGIO: I don't know! I don't know! It's driving me mad. Sympathy, you say? Do you know how I could show my **real** sympathy, here and now? By going in there to her, as she lies all innocent on her bed, and from the very love I bear her, killing her!

NELLI: Come, come, Giorgio! I understand your state of mind, but you go too far. This is unreasonable.

GIORGIO: Do you expect me to be reasonable?

NELLI: You must be!

GIORGIO: I know, I know: you have to tell me so, I know! But suppose it had happened to you—would you be reasonable?

NELLI: Of course I would! After all, it's not **her** fault, poor soul. **She's** done nothing wrong.

GIORGIO: That's just why it's so cruel for me. The crime is all the more brutal because she's innocent. It makes it worse for me—can't you see that? If she were to blame, my honour would be hurt, and I could have my revenge. But instead it's my love that's wounded. And don't you see that nothing is more cruel to my love than being compelled to feel pity?

NELLI: But surely your love ought to make you compassionate?

GIORGIO: Love can't do that.

NELLI: But that would be even more cruel . . .

GIORGIO: Yes! . . .

NELLI: . . . than what the poor girl has already suffered.

GIORGIO (*thoughtfully*): Yes, yes, that's exactly it. Not to show sympathy would be cruelty to her; but to have it is cruelty to myself.

NELLI: But surely . . .

GIORGIO: And the more you argue and the more I see the justice of your arguments, the greater grows the cruelty to me. (*A change of tone.*) Granted I mustn't be carried away by my emotions—I must reason; I must realise that she is not to blame, that physically she has been more wronged than I, and that her poor torn body is in great pain from the violence and shame; yet I can't blot out of my mind the realization that she is no longer mine alone. She has belonged to some other . . . vile wretch—and I am expected to share her love with the memory of that! Can't you see that my instinct rebels at the very idea? That if I gave way to it now instead of to my reason, I'd be even more cruel than fate has already been to her: I would **leave** her in her shame? . . . Even despise her?

NELLI: That would be ungenerous!

GIORGIO: It would be vile!

NELLI: Ah, you admit it!

GIORGIO: Yes, vile! Vile! But if love proves to be so vile when tortured by bitter jealousy—as I am now—what can I do about it? What can I do?

NELLI: Come, come, Giorgio. You're torturing yourself unnecessarily. It's the first moment of shock, you know . . .

GIORGIO: No! It's the jungle! It's the primeval forest! Once there was at least a natural horror in the primitive lusts of nature. But now . . . (*scornfully*) a public park, with its avenues and hedges and seats . . . a woman, wearing a little hat, sitting there, painting . . . and here comes the brute—dressed—smartly, of course! I can just see him—probably wearing elegant kid gloves! (*Suddenly quiet and with great sorrow in his voice at the realization.*) Oh, no . . . he couldn't have been; he scratched her with his hands; tore her poor neck . . . (*Shuddering.*) Don't you see how that makes it all the more sordid and ugly? And I'm expected to be generous, while all the time my feelings are tearing at me like wild beasts . . . Generous! (*He pauses a moment, then.*) No, no, I can't. I can't. I need to go away. Away from here.

NELLI: Why? Where? Do you really mean to say you could leave her now—like this?

GIORGIO: It would be more cruel to stay.

NELLI: But what do you mean to do? Where are you going?

GIORGIO: I need to run away from the feelings which torment me now . . . (*The bedroom door opens and* SIGNORA BETTI *and the* DOCTOR *approach.*)

SIGNORA BETTI: (*anxiously*): Giorgio . . . Giorgio . . . Laura's asking for you. (*She suddenly curbs her anxiety at the sight of her son-in-law's overwrought state.*) What is it, Giorgio? You're so pale! Your face . . . oh my boy. My poor boy!

GIORGIO: Please . . . please. Don't come near me. Don't speak to me!

ROMERI: Signora, listen to me; don't you see that he is in no fit . . .

GIORGIO: You understand, Doctor, don't you?

ROMERI: Yes, I realise that at this moment you . . .

SIGNORA BETTI: But she's asking for him, calling for him again and again!

GIORGIO (*shrinking back*): I can't! No, I can't, I can't, I can't!

ROMERI: You see? It would do her more harm, Signora, to see him in this state, believe me. He too needs to be given time. Wait a little and you'll see that he'll become . . .

GIORGIO (*scornfully*): Are you trying to say I'll become resigned?

SIGNORA BETTI: Why resigned? Do you believe . . . Oh!

ROMERI: Come, come, Signora. We must think of him too.

SIGNORA BETTI: Yes, my son, I'm thinking of you, indeed I am! But the only cure for what you're both suffering . . .

GIORGIO: . . . Is pity! You too—just like the rest of them! Pity!

SIGNORA BETTI: Yes, pity—for one another. That's how I see it, and I'm only a poor ignorant woman. Pity—not resignation to an evil that doesn't exist.

GIORGIO: How can you say that?

SIGNORA BETTI: No, it does not exist. And your love should tell you so—you really love my daughter! If you don't, what **do** you love? Isn't that so, Doctor? (*Appealing*) Signor Nelli?

GIORGIO (*his voice deep with anguish*): I did love her—oh, so much. But just because I loved her so much . . . Oh, how can I make you understand? Before I **could** pity the girl I loved—but not any longer, not now.

SIGNORA BETTI (*misunderstanding*): You don't love her any longer? Why?

GIORGIO: Don't you see—if I am to pity her . . . (*He breaks off.*) But what pity can I show? And can your pity or mine help **me**? I need to be cruel—do you think it's because I don't love your daughter? No, it's because I **do** love her!

SIGNORA BETTI: It's not true; it's not true. You can't love her like that!

GIORGIO: Do you think my love can be like yours? Or that the situation is the same for you as it is for me? You **cannot** feel as I do!

SIGNORA BETTI: But she's calling for you. What do you propose to do?

GIORGIO: Nothing. I must go away, I must go away!

SIGNORA BETTI: And you're going to desert her like this?

ROMERI: Perhaps Signora it would after all be best if he did go away for a time.

SIGNORA BETTI: But can she stay alone like that in there, if she knows he's gone away?

ROMERI: **You** could stay with her.

NELLI: Ah, that might be a solution.

SIGNORA BETTI: But who's going to tell her? If you have the courage to leave her, Giorgio, you ought also to have the courage to tell her.

GIORGIO (*resolutely*): You really wish me to tell her?

ROMERI: No, for Heaven's sake, Signora!

SIGNORA BETTI: Well, I hope you realise that my daughter may die when she finds herself deserted at a time like this by the one who ought to be nearest to her, if he had any heart!

ROMERI: No, no! It's not that, Signora.

NELLI: If he cannot control himself **now**, perhaps . . .

GIORGIO: For me it's all finished. Finished. I can find in myself enough pity to stay—but you realise, I suppose that if I do—it's solely for the sake of appearances. I'll stay—but it will only make matters worse.

NELLI: No, no. You'll see, Giorgio . . .

GIORGIO: What shall I see?

NELLI: You'll see that . . . No, I don't want to say anything to you now, because I know that at this moment every word would be a wound for you. By the way, Signora—you said you had to see to your husband, didn't you? May I suggest that you go home then?

SIGNORA BETTI: But . . . how **can** I?

NELLI: Go home and don't worry. Giorgio is staying.

GIORGIO: Only for the sake of appearances!

NELLI: Very well—for the sake of appearances. (*Quietly— aside to her.*) It's best to leave husband and wife alone for a while, Signora. (*Raising his voice again.*) He's going to change his clothes now, and then he'll come and spend the evening with me.

SIGNORA BETTI: What about Laura?

ROMERI: She must not be disturbed. You go and tell her that I have ordered her husband to keep away from her.

SIGNORA BETTI: But if she's left alone she'll go mad.

ROMERI: No, Signora. You'll find she'll sleep with the sedative I've given her to calm her nerves. She's probably asleep already—perhaps you'd go and see.

SIGNORA BETTI: Yes, all right, I'll go.

ROMERI: And now—I must be going too. Good-bye, Signor Banti. You know, one must always be stronger than the blow that strikes one.

GIORGIO (*quietly*): This blow is worse than her death for me. Can you imagine what it will be like tomorrow, Doctor?— Laura—no longer the Laura I knew—lying there, looking at me . . .

SIGNORA BETTI (*approaching joyfully*): Yes, yes. She's fast asleep.

ROMERI: Ah, what did I tell you?

SIGNORA BETTI: Well, I'm going now—I really must. I'll be here tomorrow morning. Good-bye, Giorgio, and . . . well, I won't say anything more to you now, my boy.

GIORGIO: Good-bye.

NELLI: I'll see you home, Signora. Shall I come back for you, Giorgio?

GIORGIO: No, no—I may come to your place—later on. I'll see.

NELLI: Just as you like. I shall be at home. Good-bye. Come then, Signora. Doctor. (GIORGIO *is silent for a moment, contemplating the catastrophe that has overwhelmed him. Then, quietly—thinking aloud.*)

GIORGIO: Perhaps I should go to her . . . yes, if she's asleep, I could look at her without her knowing . . . and that way, perhaps . . . No, no—I can't do it. I can't. I can't! (*He rings for the manservant. After a moment,* MANFREDI *enters.*)

MANFREDI: Signore?

GIORGIO: Tell Antonio to get the car out. I'm going to the villa at Monteporzio.

MANFREDI: Alone, Signore?

GIORGIO: Yes, alone—right now! Pack a case for me, will you?

MANFREDI: Very good, Signore. (GIORGIO *is about to go when* LAURA *appears in the bedroom doorway. She is pale in a violet dressing-gown with a silk veil round her neck.*)

LAURA: Giorgio. Giorgio . . .

GIORGIO: Laura! I thought you were asleep.

LAURA: No—I heard you call for Manfredi. You're not . . . leaving me, are you? You don't answer me, Giorgio, why do you stare at me like that? I can see horror—and, yes—disgust in your eyes. (*Never raising her voice.*) Don't, Giorgio, don't—that would kill me. (*There is longing behind her words, longing for him to clasp her to him.*) If you want me to live, then you must help me to blot out of my mind what has happened today. I need your love, Giorgio. Only that can make me whole and pure again: and I want to be pure—for you, Giorgio, do you understand? For you. Oh, Giorgio—say something; come nearer to me . . . please. Show me that you do love me—or kill me if you must—but wipe out this shame that's upon me. I would happily die if that's the only way. Giorgio? Giorgio? (*There is a great plea in the way she calls his name. A pause.*)

GIORGIO (*drunk with her nearness, suddenly full of tenderness and love*): Laura . . . Laura . . . forgive me. Forgive me! My love.

LAURA (*very quietly and gently—almost like a prayer*): Thank you. Dear God—thank you.

ACT II

Part of the garden in front of the Banti's villa at Monteporzio. The villa with a colonnaded porch is on the left. There are trees at the back and on the right. It is autumn.

   LAURA, *in a chaise-longue, pale, rather weak with the feverish languor of unexhausted passion, listens with interest, and at the same time perturbed, to what the old gardener is saying to her as he stands near her with his knapsack, a bundle of cuttings*

under his arm, and his grafting knife in his hand. A nightingale's
song is heard off, followed by an answering call.

FILIPPO: Ah, yes, Signora Banti—but you must have the
   knack! If you haven't got the knack, you can try to give life
   to a plant, but it'll die.
LAURA: Can the plant die of it, too?
FILIPPO: Why yes, of course. You prepare the plant—the stock
   we call it—by cutting it . . . we'll say cross-wise (that's the
   splice graft.) Then there's the saddle graft, and the cleft, and
   the crown . . . oh, there's lots of ways of grafting. Then you
   push in a bud, or one of these here shoots you see. You bind
   it up firmly; then you cover it all up with mud or wax,
   whichever you like. You think you've made a graft, and you
   wait. But what's the good of waiting? You've killed the stock!
   The knack, that's what you want. Ah, perhaps you think it
   dies because the job's been done by a clumsy old gardener
   who would hurt you, Lord save us, if he touched you with his
   rough hands. But these great, clumsy hands . . . Look here:
   I'll show you. (*He fetches a big pot in which a leafy plant is
   growing and brings it over to* LAURA.) See the plant in this
   pot here?—A beauty, eh? It's a pleasure to look at it, isn't
   it?—But only to look at, mind! It doesn't give you any fruit.
   Then I come along, with my great clumsy gardener's hands,
   and . . . well, just you watch me. (*He begins to take off the
   leaves to prepare the graft, fitting the words to the action and
   finishing both simultaneously.*) See? I begin by stripping off
   the leaves. It looks as though I'm destroying your plant,
   doesn't it? There: now I've stripped off most of its leaves;
   now I cut it,—now I make an incision—wait a bit . . . there!—
   And without your knowing anything about it, I've made it
   bear fruit for you. Do you know how I did it? I took a bud
   from another plant and I grafted it onto this one. It's August,
   isn't it? Well, next spring you'll have the fruit. D'you know
   what they call this sort of grafting?
LAURA (*smiling sadly*): No, I don't.
FILIPPO: Shut-eye. That's it, 'shut-eye grafting', what's done
   in August, that's what we call this: because, you see, there's

the 'open-eye' too, what's done in May, when the bud can break open immediately.

LAURA (*with infinite sadness*): But the ... stock—what about that?

FILIPPO: Ah, the stock. Yes, well **that's** got to be in sap, Signora—always. Because if the sap isn't rising the graft doesn't take.

LAURA: In sap? I don't understand.

FILIPPO: In sap. That means—how shall I put it? Well—in love, that's it: in love. Because it wants, it ... 'desires', the fruit it can't give on its own.

LAURA (*with lively interest*): It wants to make this fruit its own? Through its own love?

FILIPPO: Through its own roots that have to feed the fruit. Through its own branches that have to bear it.

LAURA (*thoughtfully*): Through its love ... yes, its love. Without knowing or remembering how that bud came to it, it makes it its own ... through its love.

FILIPPO: That's it, Signora: that's the way it is.

ZENA (*calling, off*): Filippo! Filippo!

FILIPPO: Ah, there's Zena with her little boy. I'll go and open the gate for them. (*Going.*) Excuse me, Signora. (*He exits to the right, among the trees.*)

LAURA (*remains absorbed; then gets up, goes to the recently grafted tree, and puts her head among its leaves, repeating to herself slowly with the anguish of intense, desperate desire*): Through its love! Through its love! (*Sound of an iron gate being opened off.*)

FILIPPO (*off*): Come in, come in. What are you afraid of? (*He re-enters right, followed by* ZENA, *who is dressed in the fashion of the country women of the Roman countryside.*) Here she is. She's shy, the silly girl!

ZENA: No, I'm not. Why should I be shy? Good morning, Signora.

LAURA: Good morning. (*Pause. Far off the nightingale is heard again.*)

LAURA: So you are Zena?

ZENA: Yes, Signora.

FILIPPO: D'you see how old and ugly she's got?

LAURA: No, why?

ZENA: We're poor folk, Signora.

LAURA: How old are you? You can't be more than twenty-five!

ZENA (*after a moment*): Yes, I know why you stare at me, Signora. But then your kind don't know what we poor country women have to go through—so I suppose I can't blame you for looking surprised.

FILIPPO: Now, now, Zena . . .

ZENA: But as for you, Filippo—you ugly old monster, trying to play the 'gentleman' here in the villa . . .

FILIPPO: Well, I like that!

ZENA: . . . **And** you're all deformed, what's more . . . What are you trying to do? Compare your worries with mine?

FILIPPO: Toh! Great worries, indeed!

ZENA: Who had five children, Signora? Did he have them?

FILIPPO (*suddenly remembering*): Ah, now I come to think of it—did you come without the boy? I told you to bring him with you because the Signora wanted to meet him.

ZENA: I didn't bring him, Signora.

LAURA: Why didn't you?

ZENA: Well . . . because the lad's working with his father.

FILIPPO: Couldn't you have called him for a moment?

ZENA: What! Tell him in front of his father that the signora wanted him here?!

FILIPPO: Where's the harm in that?

ZENA: After all that people have been saying about—you know what!

FILIPPO: Go on with you! D'you think your husband still worries about that?

ZENA: No, he never thinks about it, unless someone puts the idea into his head. But anyway, what's this got to do with the boy coming here? What did you want with him, Signora? We've never talked about . . . that affair . . . my husband and I haven't, since then.

LAURA: I know, I know, Zena. I sent for you because I wanted to talk to you myself now—alone.

ZENA: What about?

LAURA: Go along now, Filippo. Haven't you any work to do?

FILIPPO: I'm going, Signora. But I must say one thing for Zena, though it goes against the grain—still, fair's fair! I'm old and I know all about what happened when she was in service here with the old master and mistress—when she was hardly sixteen, and the young master wasn't twenty—well, **she** wasn't the one to talk!

ZENA: That's the truth, Signora!

FILIPPO: It was her mother—her mother!

ZENA: But nobody gives it a thought now—not even my mother.

LAURA: I know, Zena. That's not what I wanted to talk to you about. Go along, Filippo.

FILIPPO: All right, all right, I'm going. Sorry, Signora, if I spoke out of turn. I'm going.

ZENA (*suddenly resentful*): Has somebody been here Signora, without my knowing, to talk about the boy?

LAURA: No Zena, I assure you—no one.

ZENA: Tell me straight, Signora, because I gave my word then, when I might have taken advantage of the position if I hadn't had a conscience—and I was the only one among the lot of them who had, you know!—And I've kept my word up to now.

LAURA: No, no, nobody's been here. Don't worry. The idea just came into my head. I remembered that before I married I was told that my husband had—well, when he was younger, here at the villa, he . . . (*She hesitates.*)

ZENA: Why do you worry yourself about that now, Signora?

LAURA: Wait! I want to know. I want to talk to you, Zena. Sit down, here by me.

ZENA: Thank you. (*She sits on the bench. After a moment, embarrassed.*) You know, Signora, it seems as if you're talking about another world now.

LAURA: Well—you were so young then.

ZENA: Oh, a silly, dreamy girl! And I didn't look as I do now, you know.

LAURA: I can imagine it—you must have been very pretty.

ZENA: I wasn't bad looking.

LAURA: And you were already engaged, weren't you?

ZENA: Yes, Signora—(*Stressing it slightly.*)— To the man I'm married to now.

LAURA: Oh.

ZENA (*shrugging her shoulders and sighing*): Well, you know how it happens, Signora . . . (*A short pause.*)

LAURA (*almost timidly*): And did . . . he know it?

ZENA (*impudently, but without immodesty*): Who? The young master?

LAURA: Yes—did he know you were engaged?

ZENA: Yes, Signora, of course he knew it. But he was only a boy himself . . .

LAURA: Yes, but tell me . . .

ZENA: Signora, I'm a poor woman—but believe me, if I did any harm then, I did it only to myself, and I certainly didn't want any unnecessary harm to come to others.

LAURA: I believe you, Zena. I'm sure you didn't. But tell me, because I want to know: you said 'unnecessary'; were you really so sure of it, then?

ZENA: Sure of what? That the child wasn't the young master's?

LAURA: Yes, because—it sometimes happens, you know—you might have been doubtful about it yourself.

ZENA (*she rises. A little angrily*): Why are you talking to me like this, Signora?

LAURA: Please don't be upset. Sit down, sit down.

ZENA: No, I won't, Signora! It's not for you to . . .

LAURA: I should like to know, Zena, because . . . because I should be . . . **glad** if you told me that . . .

ZENA: That the child **was** the young master's?

LAURA: Are you absolutely certain?

ZENA (*sharply*): Now listen, Signora . . .

LAURA (*anxiously*): Tell me, tell me!

ZENA: I think you ought to be satisfied with what I've always said.

LAURA: If you're absolutely sure of it . . .

ZENA: Careful, Signora: remember that poverty sometimes makes one say . . .

LAURA (*interrupting*): No, Zena—you're too honest to lie to me. It's to your conscience I'm appealing now.

ZENA: You can leave my conscience out of it. It's always been perfectly clear. It made me say what I had to say then, and I'm not going to back on it now.

LAURA: But was it your conscience? That's what I need to know, or was it only because you were afraid . . .

ZENA (*with a scornful laugh*): You talk just like my mother did when she heard about the young master. 'You're too young,' she said—'too "inexperienced"!' 'Did I know for sure,' she said, 'or was I denying the whole thing because I was afraid?'

LAURA: Your mother thought as I do, you see!

ZENA: But I can understand **my mother** talking like that. I'd already done the harm to myself—with the other man.

LAURA: With your fiancé?

ZENA: Yes, he knew that I was going to have a baby and he wanted to take advantage of the young master. But why do you come to me **now**, Signora—after nine years—to dig up the whole affair?

LAURA: Because . . . I know . . . well, I know that your husband demanded a large dowry to marry you.

ZENA: Oh, I see! But he wasn't poor at all, Signora. My mother annoyed him by telling everybody about the young master. He didn't want to marry me any more, though he knew perfectly well the child was his own . . . But there was money to be stung from the young master's people up here at the villa, and he wanted to get his share of it. And I warn you that if he gets to know that it would **please** you if I still had some doubt in my mind—God knows why . . .

LAURA: Oh, you make me sorry I ever wanted to talk the matter over frankly with you because of a scruple you couldn't even understand!

ZENA: Who knows? Perhaps I do understand you, Signora! You needn't be sorry you spoke.

LAURA: What do you understand?

ZENA (*smiling*): We're not fools out here in the country. I see that it would please you if your husband had had a child by me. Well, I'll tell you just this: I bore the child to the man who was his real father! (*The gate opens—off.*)

ZENA (*a little nervous*): Oh, here is the young master.

LAURA (*running to meet him*): Giorgio . . . Giorgio . . . Oh, Giorgio.

GIORGIO (*apprehensively*): What's the matter? What is it, Laura?

LAURA: Nothing . . . nothing.

GIORGIO: But you're crying.

LAURA: No—it's nothing.

GIORGIO: Nothing? What has happened?

LAURA: Nothing, I tell you. It's the surprise, I suppose— I didn't expect you back so soon.

ZENA: I'd better be going, Signora. Good-bye.

LAURA: Yes, yes, Zena, you may go. Good-bye. (ZENA *exits right*.)

GIORGIO (*surprised, pained*): What's this? You've been talking to . . . Did she come to tell you something about . . . ?

LAURA (*abruptly, strongly denying*): No, no. She didn't tell me anything.

GIORGIO: Why did she come here then?

LAURA: I sent for her.

GIORGIO: You sent for her? Why?

LAURA: Oh, out of curiosity . . . Just a whim.

GIORGIO: That was foolish, Laura. You oughtn't to have done it.

LAURA: Filippo mentioned her—you know, just casually— and I felt I wanted to see her . . . and the boy, too. But she didn't bring him. And, seeing that she was here . . .

GIORGIO: . . . She told you, no doubt . . .

LAURA: Nothing, absolutely nothing. Anyway, you know she always denied everything.

GIORGIO: Hm! Why, they wanted to blackmail me!

LAURA: **She** didn't! It was her mother: she told me so just now.

GIORGIO: Why were you crying, then?

LAURA: Not because of her—it had nothing to do with her! I told you, I don't really know why—it just happened, as soon as I saw you unexpectedly like that—(*Quietly*) And . . . because of what I feel, Giorgio. But I'm laughing now, can't you see? Because I've got you back with me again.

GIORGIO: But . . . you said yourself that you didn't expect me back so soon.

LAURA: Yes, that's true. But I was so lonely, Giorgio, so terribly lonely. I need you so much! . . . To hold me tight like this, and never go away from me again, never, never!

GIORGIO: But it was for your sake I went, Laura, darling.

LAURA: Yes, I know you did, Giorgio.

GIORGIO: How cold your little hands are. Here, I've brought you a shawl to keep you warm.

LAURA: Thank you, Giorgio. I'm so glad we decided to run away here, suddenly—on the spur of the moment.

GIORGIO: But how quickly time flies. It's more than a month ago now—and the cold weather has come.

LAURA: But we'll stay on here. It'll be nicer here now, absolutely alone. You aren't afraid of the cold, are you?

GIORGIO: No, dear.

LAURA: You must never be afraid with me.

GIORGIO (*smiling*): But I've been afraid **of** you, dear.

LAURA: Don't call me 'dear' like that!

GIORGIO: What do you want me to call you?

LAURA: Laura—in your own special way.

GIORGIO: All right—Laura.

LAURA: That's better. I love the way you say my name.

GIORGIO: Why?

LAURA: I don't know. I like to watch your lips while you say it.

GIORGIO: Laura, mine.

LAURA: Yes, yours, yours. You can't imagine how much I'm yours now. And yet I should like to be even more.

GIORGIO: Darling.

LAURA: But it's impossible. You know don't you, that I can't possibly be more yours than I am?

GIORGIO: Yes, Laura.

LAURA: If I loved you any more I should die. But I should like to die for that.

GIORGIO: What are you saying?

LAURA: For my own sake, I mean: so as not to be—I don't know—a being that seems to be still living the least little bit for itself; but to be something belonging to you—something you can make even more yours, utterly yours, through your love. Do you understand?

GIORGIO (*quietly*): Yes, Laura, I do understand.

LAURA: You feel it, don't you? You feel that I am all yours through your love? And that for myself I have nothing, nothing; not a thought, not a memory of anything any longer. I am completely yours . . . through you . . . because of your love.

NOTE: LAURA has spoken these words with the most absorbed intensity. Almost, as it were, the sap of the plant the gardener spoke to her about. She becomes very pale and a strange smile appears on her face; a smile that melts away as she is about to faint.

GIORGIO: My darling, you're trembling. Laura. Laura, are you ill?

LAURA (*quietly*): Let me rest my head on your chest a moment—near your heart.

GIORGIO: What's the matter?

LAURA: Nothing . . . nothing . . . (*A moment's pause. The nightingale is heard again, followed a moment later by an answering call further off.*)

LAURA (*quietly*): There.

GIORGIO: I thought you were going to faint, Laura. You've grown quite pale.

LAURA: No, it's nothing.

GIORGIO: You're cold. Sit down, my darling.

LAURA: No, no . . . Don't help me. You don't understand.

GIORGIO: What?

LAURA: That it's like this. Like this!

GIORGIO: What's like this?

LAURA (*an intense whisper*): That I am like this only because of your love.

GIORGIO (*puzzled by her tone*): Are you feeling all right, Laura? You sound so strange.

LAURA: I've touched it here on your breast . . . for an instant, I've reached it.

GIORGIO: What?

LAURA: With your love and mine, just for an instant, here on your breast, I've attained . . . life!

GIORGIO: What do you mean?

LAURA (*a violent shudder shakes her whole body*): Oh God!

GIORGIO (*alarmed*): Laura—you frighten me. What **is** the matter?

LAURA: Nothing. I'm rather cold. I feel a little bewildered . . .

GIORGIO: You must rest my darling. You're over-excited.

LAURA (*suddenly, with almost heroic ardour*): Yes, I know— but that's how I want it to be.

GIORGIO: I don't understand you; (*tenderly*) but I do know that it's bad for you to be like this. (*Puzzled*) You look so strange: happy—yet you seem to be suffering.

LAURA: Do I?

GIORGIO: Yes. And I won't have you suffer, do you understand, Laura? Not in any way—because I love you, dearly.

LAURA (*drinking in the sweetness of his words*): Do you, Giorgio?

GIORGIO: Yes. (*A moment's pause.*) Laura, why do you look at me like that? Your eyes . . .

LAURA (*almost provocatively*): My eyes? Tell me . . . go on, say it!

GIORGIO: My God, Laura!

LAURA (*laughing, gay*): Look into my eyes: look! Can't you see yourself there?

GIORGIO: You're making fun of me!

LAURA: No, no, I'm quite serious.

GIORGIO: But I don't . . .

LAURA: All right, I won't laugh. Let's be calm now. Sit down . . . here by me. I'll make room for you. (*She sits on the chaise-longue.*)

GIORGIO: No, if we're to be serious, I'll sit here on the bench.

LAURA: No, here. And I'll sit like this—on your knee. (*She does so.*) Tell me, did you go to see Mother?

GIORGIO: Yes, but she wasn't in.

LAURA: Wasn't Giulietta there?

GIORGIO: No, she'd gone out with your mother.

LAURA: Didn't the maid give you a message?

GIORGIO: No, nothing. Why?

LAURA: Because I rang Mother up from here.

GIORGIO: You telephoned? This morning?

LAURA: Yes.

GIORGIO: To speak to me? Did you want me to bring you back something?

LAURA: No. I didn't feel very well.

GIORGIO: Oh? When?

LAURA: Just after you left. When I got up. But it wasn't anything much—it soon passed off.

GIORGIO: What was it?

LAURA: Nothing, I tell you. I just felt dizzy as soon as I got up. Only for a moment, you know—as I did just now.

GIORGIO: And you rang up to ask Mother to send the doctor?

LAURA: No. I didn't want a doctor—I wanted you. To tell you to come back quickly. Mother did say she wanted to send Dr Romeri with you, but . . .

GIORGIO: Nobody told me anything about it.

LAURA: All the better! It was Mother's idea. I didn't like it—I told her a dozen times there was no need for a doctor. But you know what Mother's like. I am afraid we shall have her turning up here at any moment with Dr Romeri.

GIORGIO: And a good thing, too. Then he'll see . . .

LAURA: No, no! What is there for him to see? I wanted **you** to come back quickly. You're back—and that's enough.

GIORGIO: But perhaps the doctor . . .

LAURA: What do you think the doctor can do for me? I warn you: if he comes I shan't let him see me!

GIORGIO: But why?

LAURA: Because I don't want him to. I'll hide myself—under your jacket—like this; and he'll have to be content with just hearing my voice. (GEORGIO *laughs*.)

LAURA: I'll tell him . . . (*She stops*.)

GIORGIO: That it's my fault?

LAURA (*after a moment*): Wait!

GIORGIO (*amused*): What are you up to now?

LAURA: I can hear your heart beating. A strong, slow beat; and a tiny little quick beat!

GIORGIO: What are you talking about?

LAURA: Your heart and your watch!

GIORGIO: What a wonderful discovery!

LAURA: **Can** they be measuring the same time? My heart is certainly beating faster than yours. Oh! What a horrid heart it is!

GIORGIO (*laughing*): Mine horrid? Why?

LAURA: I've never heard your heart beating before. It's so wretchedly calm and slow.

GIORGIO: How ought it to beat?

LAURA: How? Well—if I knew that you were listening to mine, it . . . it would beat so fast that it would burst! But yours—not a bit faster! Quite unaffected!

GIORGIO: Naturally—when you talk of a nice doctor you don't want to see!

LAURA: Not to see . . . just to complain to—about you!

GIORGIO: Yes—with your face hidden! Because you know quite well that I'm not responsible! (*Almost before he finishes these words he becomes greatly upset, as though the words, referring to what Laura is suffering, have suddenly acquired a new meaning for him, one that he did not intend to give them.*) No . . . I didn't mean that! I . . .

LAURA: You are not responsible? What do you mean?

GIORGIO (*with ever increasing agitation*): No, I . . .

LAURA (*she rises from his knee*): Giorgio, what are you worrying about?

GIORGIO: Oh, my God! Nothing! (*Then, in a hollow voice.*) Do you think Dr Romeri will come?

LAURA: I don't know. Why?

GIORGIO: Because it'll be a good thing if he does. I want him to.

LAURA: But, good Heavens, Giorgio, I was only joking.

GIORGIO: I know, I know!

LAURA: Do you think I would complain about you, except as a joke?

GIORGIO: Oh no, Laura! **That** doesn't worry me.

LAURA: What is it, then?

GIORGIO: Well . . . if you're not well . . .

LAURA: No, no. There's nothing the matter with me—I have you, and that's all I need. Everything else I have comes to me from you—joy, sorrow, death—all from you! Because I'm entirely as you want me to be, as I want to be—all yours! Surely you can see that that's everything—you must know that!

GIORGIO: Yes, yes.

LAURA: Well, then—that's all there is to it. Now can I be ill? I . . . (*She suddenly gasps, as though she felt unsteady.*) Ah! Hold me, Giorgio.

GIORGIO: Do you see? And you pretend there's nothing the matter!

LAURA: No, I'm just a little tired . . . Give me your arm.

FILIPPO (*calling, off*): Signora, Signora. Your mother's coming, with another gentleman.

GIORGIO: Ah, that'll be the doctor.

LAURA: No, no, Giorgio! I don't want to see him.

GIORGIO: But I want you to see him.

LAURA: No, no. Please take him away—take him into the house. I'm not going to let him see me. (SIGNORA BETTI *enters.*)

SIGNORA BETTI: Good morning, Giorgio.

GIORGIO: Good morning. Where's the doctor?

SIGNORA BETTI: He's just coming.

LAURA: No, please, Giorgio—take him indoors. Please, **please**!

GIORGIO: Oh, very well. (*He exits.*)

SIGNORA BETTI: What's the matter, Laura?

LAURA (*excited*): Oh, you shouldn't have done it, Mother, you shouldn't!

SIGNORA BETTI: What?

LAURA: You shouldn't have brought the doctor! You have done wrong, wrong! You've no idea how wrong!

SIGNORA BETTI: But why? You told me on the telephone that you'd been feeling ill.

LAURA: There's nothing the matter with me, nothing!

SIGNORA BETTI: Even so, there was no harm in . . .

LAURA: No harm you say! Do you think a doctor can understand or know what I feel? Do you think medicine is what I need?

SIGNORA BETTI: But surely, if you say there's nothing wrong . . .

LAURA: There **is** nothing wrong. I will not have it thought of as a wrong—do you understand?

SIGNORA BETTI: But . . .

LAURA: And by bringing that doctor here, Giorgio is bound to look on it as something wrong . . . (*Almost breaking down.*) Like the wrong that was done to me before!

SIGNORA BETTI: You don't . . . you don't mean . . . ? What are you trying to say, Laura? (*She gasps.*) Surely you can't be going to . . .

LAURA: Yes, yes, Mother! Yes!

SIGNORA BETTI: Oh, my God! And what about him—your husband? Does he know?

LAURA: That's why I say you've done wrong, Mother.

SIGNORA BETTI: I?

LAURA: Yes. That he should know of it first from the doctor: that way he'll think of it as something . . . evil . . . for which there is only one remedy: a remedy more hateful than the disease!

SIGNORA BETTI: But if you say that . . . that it was he . . .

LAURA: No, it wasn't! It wasn't! I know it wasn't! I feel it.

SIGNORA BETTI: How do you know? What is it you feel? I'm afraid you're over-excited, Laura, and that . . .

LAURA: You think I'm raving? (*Quietly, in a deep tone.*) I can't explain it to you logically, but I realised it here just now, Mother; I **know** that it is so, that it cannot be otherwise.

SIGNORA BETTI: What do you mean, my child? I don't understand you. What cannot be otherwise?

LAURA: This, Mother! This that I feel. Reason doesn't tell me; perhaps reason can't admit it. But nature knows. My body knows. (*A change of tone.*) A plant—one of these plants

here—knows that it could not exist without love. Filippo
explained it to me just now. Even a plant cannot exist if it's
not in love. Do you see how it is?

SIGNORA BETTI: But my child, you're . . .

LAURA: No, I'm not over-excited, Mother! And I'm quite sure
of this—that in my poor body—when it happened—in my
poor torn flesh, Mother, there must have been love! And if
there was love, it could not have been for anyone but my
husband. (*With a triumphant, almost joyful tone.*) That is why
it's not evil . . . not wrong!

SIGNORA BETTI: What are you saying? Oh, this is a new
torture, my child! Are you certain of it, absolutely certain?

LAURA: Yes, but it's as I have just said: it **must** be like that.

SIGNORA BETTI: But what about Giorgio? Does he know?

LAURA: I think he knows already. But now, with that doctor
here . . . Oh! This is just what shouldn't have happened, don't
you see—that he should get to know it in this way?

SIGNORA BETTI: But if you say he knows already, why
then . . . ?

LAURA: I wanted him to feel the same way as I do about it, I
wanted him to understand it as I do, to make himself and me
so much one person that he would feel and wish in me and
with me what I feel and wish!

SIGNORA BETTI: Good heavens, Laura! I really am afraid
that you . . .

GIORGIO (*off. Calling*): Laura.

LAURA: Hush! Here they are . . . Let's go in. (*Going.*) I won't
see him, I **won't**!

GIORGIO (*calling*): Laura . . . Laura . . .

LAURA (*calling back*): No, Giorgio. I told you I wouldn't!
Come along, Mother! (*She drags her mother away.*)

After a moment, GIORGIO *speaks on an approach continuing
gravely but calmly and composedly his conversation with the*
DOCTOR.

GIORGIO: You see Doctor, it's as I was telling you; I gave in
then. I controlled myself, as I had to . . . but it was torture!

Perhaps even to you, Doctor, my violence seemed . . .

ROMERI (*interrupting*): No, for my part . . .

GIORGIO: . . . If not to you, then to others, it might have seemed excessive. But then they weren't in a position to feel as I did about it.

ROMERI: Everyone has his own way of feeling about things, you know!

GIORGIO: But if my first reaction **was** rather violent—it was partly directed against myself. Can you understand that, Doctor?

ROMERI (*sympathetically*): I think so.

GIORGIO: Because you see, as soon as I saw her, as soon as she came in to me from her room, all my anger and violence dropped from me at once, and I took her into my arms—not out of pity, no! But because I felt I **had** to . . . because I loved her. And I swear to you that I've never given another thought to it since; not once. For a month we've been together here, like a young couple on their honeymoon. (*Changing his tone.*) But now, Doctor, if **this** is true . . . (*He stops.*)

ROMERI: Ah, I understand.

GIORGIO: To recover from one blow—well, I've managed that! But a second—no!

ROMERI: Well, let's still hope it is not as you think.

GIORGIO: I don't know, but I'm afraid it is! And if it were . . . do you understand me, Doctor?

ROMERI: Yes, I understand.

GIORGIO: Please go, then, and tell Laura that if it turns out as I fear, (*Slowly, enunciating clearly, almost syllable by syllable.*) I shall not be able to accept a compromise. Go and tell her that. I'll wait here.

The DOCTOR *is about to speak, then thinks better of it, and with a shrug, he exits.* GIORGIO *remains standing, deep in thought, torn by conflicting emotions. He passes his hand across his forehead as if to wipe away his thought as*

THE CURTAIN FALLS

ACT III

*A room in the villa. Doors to the left, right and centre. A window
on the left. It is immediately after Act Two. When the curtain
rises* ROMERI *is alone, waiting near the door on the right.*
SIGNORA BETTI *enters.*

SIGNORA BETTI: I'm sorry, Doctor, but it's no use: she absolutely refuses to see you.

ROMERI: Does she know her husband wishes her to?

SIGNORA BETTI: I told her so, but it only made her more
   irritable.

ROMERI: Why?

SIGNORA BETTI: She got annoyed with me too, on the telephone this morning, when I told her that I would bring you
   here.

ROMERI: That's strange.

SIGNORA BETTI: She says there's no need for you to see her.

ROMERI (*with pleasant surprise, as though relieved of a great
   weight*): Ah! So there's no need!

SIGNORA BETTI: Apparently she told Giorgio the same thing
   out there in the garden.

ROMERI: Good. Then let's go and tell your son-in-law straight
   away—he's very worried, you know.

SIGNORA BETTI: Wait, Doctor! You say Giorgio is worried.
   What about?

ROMERI: Well . . . surely you understand, Signora!

SIGNORA BETTI: Oh, if that's the reason, then I'm afraid
   there can be no doubt.

ROMERI (*now puzzled*): Oh? How do you mean?

SIGNORA BETTI: She's convinced she is going to have a
   child.

ROMERI: I see. In that case . . .

SIGNORA BETTI: Has Giorgio formed the suspicion that . . .

ROMERI: Well, of course, Signora.

SIGNORA BETTI: But why?

ROMERI: Because . . . because my dear Signora Betti, it's a
   suspicion that might occur to you . . . to me . . . to anybody!

SIGNORA BETTI: Ah, but—if you don't mind my saying so—that's no reason for being certain.

ROMERI: The doubt is enough, Signora Betti.

SIGNORA BETTI: What if my daughter hasn't any?

ROMERI: Say rather that she doesn't want to have any!

SIGNORA BETTI: Exactly! She absolutely refuses to doubt.

ROMERI: Ah—if it were simply a matter of will . . . !

SIGNORA BETTI: So you too, Doctor believe that . . .

ROMERI: What I believe is beside the point, Signora. Your daughter ought to have inspired her husband with her own certainty. It seems she hasn't succeeded. The very fact that she has hidden her condition from him up to now seems to me to show that the suspicion occurred to her too.

SIGNORA BETTI: No. She hadn't meant to hide anything. She realized her condition only this morning.

ROMERI: Then why does she refuse to let me examine her if her husband wants me to?

SIGNORA BETTI: Surely you can understand why, Doctor? It's only natural for her to feel as she does.

ROMERI: It hardly seems so to me. Does she expect her husband to think it 'only natural', too?

SIGNORA BETTI: Yes.

ROMERI: I'm afraid, Signora, your daughter expects too much.

SIGNORA BETTI: She doesn't expect anything, Doctor. The fact is she cannot admit . . .

ROMERI: You mean, she won't . . .

SIGNORA BETTI: Doesn't it seem natural to you that she won't? It's repugnant to her to admit.

ROMERI: Yes, I understand. But you, too, must understand, Signora, that doubt—even the remotest doubt—is repugnant to her husband. All the more so because, as you must realize, this doubt is increased by the fact that in seven years of marriage they have had no children.

SIGNORA BETTI: Yes, that's true. Oh, my goodness, what are we to do?

ROMERI: You must try to make your daughter see that.

SIGNORA BETTI: I?

ROMERI: Your son-in-law told me that on this point he feels

he cannot compromise. He seemed quite adamant.

SIGNORA BETTI: But then . . . what about you, Doctor?

ROMERI: Me? (*He pauses.*) Signora, you probably know that
I was an army doctor, and that I resigned my commission?

SIGNORA BETTI: Yes, I did know that.

ROMERI: But do you know why I resigned?

SIGNORA BETTI: No.

ROMERI: Because in our profession, in Italy we are given
duties without corresponding rights.

SIGNORA BETTI: What do you mean, Doctor?

ROMERI: I mean, Signora, that I found myself on one occasion—(and that was enough for me)—confronted by a case
in which the execution of my duty would I felt, have been
absolutely monstrous!

SIGNORA BETTI: Oh, yes, you are right, it would be monstrous, but . . .

ROMERI: No, Signora, you don't understand in what sense I
mean it. It may be the very opposite of what you think. A
soldier in barracks—it's many years ago now—fired at his
superior officer in a fit of anger, and killed him. Then he
turned the weapon against himself. He was fatally wounded.
Well, Signora, in a case like that no one thinks of the doctor
whose job it is to save the wounded man—if he can. He is
thought of as a scientific instrument and nothing more; as
though a doctor hadn't a human being's conscience to judge
whether, for example, contrary to the duty placed on him to
save, he hasn't the right **not** to do so—or at least the right to
dispose afterwards of the life which he has restored to the
boy. That boy had taken it in order to punish himself already
with the greatest of punishments: suicide! No, the doctor's
duty is to save, even against the man's own determination to
die. And suppose I do restore him to life, what happens then?
For what purpose do I give him back his life? So that he can
then be put to death in cold blood by the very society that
denies me any right to be guided in my work by my conscience! I tell you this, Signora, so that you may understand
that I have always acknowledged, and **will** always acknowledge in all my professional cases, both the duties imposed

on me, and also the rights my conscience claims.

SIGNORA BETTI: Then you would be prepared to . . . ?

ROMERI: Yes, Signora, without the slightest hesitation—always supposing, of course, that your daughter would consent. (GIORGIO *has appeared in the centre doorway during the last speech of the* DOCTOR *and has been listening.*)

GIORGIO: And what might she not consent to?

SIGNORA BETTI: Oh, Giorgio. I hadn't noticed you come in.

GIORGIO: What might Laura not consent to, Doctor?

SIGNORA BETTI: No, no! We don't know yet, Giorgio.

GIORGIO: But is it sure, then, Doctor?

ROMERI: It seems so.

GIORGIO: And what does Laura say?

ROMERI: I haven't seen her yet.

SIGNORA BETTI (*to calm him, almost supplicating*): Perhaps Giorgio, she thinks that . . .

GIORGIO (*suddenly, interrupting her*): Thinks! Thinks what? If she is sure how can she still hesitate to give her consent? I insist on it.

ROMERI (*annoyed, even indignant*): No, no! Forgive me, but . . .

GIORGIO: I insist! I insist!

ROMERI (*stern, curt*): You cannot insist on it like this!

GIORGIO: Why not?

ROMERI: Because **she** must give the word of her own accord. I would not undertake it—nor would anybody else—otherwise.

GIORGIO: What I can't understand is why she hasn't already asked you to do it.

SIGNORA BETTI: For you it seems very simple, Giorgio: all you have to do is to say 'go ahead', but for a woman it's no easy decision.

GIORGIO: But for her own sake she ought to demand it instantly—at all costs! It ought to be nothing to her when she considers the full horror of her present position. Does she really think that I could shut my eyes to such a thing a second time? Can she expect me to forget—or pretend it doesn't exist? No, no! Where is she? Where is she?

SIGNORA BETTI (*trying to stop him*): No, Giorgio, for

heaven's sake don't go to her now.

ROMERI (*firmly*): Not like this!

GIORGIO: What does Laura say? (LAURA *enters unnoticed.*)

GIORGIO: May I at least know what she says? Or perhaps she wants me to think that her love . . . (*He breaks off as he becomes aware of* LAURA's *presence.*)

LAURA: . . . That my love? (*A moment's pause, full of suspense.*) Go on! Finish what you were saying, Giorgio.

GIORGIO: Laura, I want you to tell me at once that you're not against . . .

LAURA: Against what?

SIGNORA BETTI (*quietly, urgently*): She doesn't know what you're talking about—we haven't spoken to her yet.

GIORGIO: Then please let me explain matters to her myself.

LAURA: Yes, that would be better.

GIORGI: Wait in the next room for a few minutes please, Doctor.

LAURA (*suddenly, severely*): You too, Mother!

ROMERI: Come, Signora. (*The* DOCTOR *and* SIGNORA BETTI *exit centre. A pause.*)

LAURA: You were discussing my love, just like that, in front of . . .

GIORGIO (*completing the sentence*): . . . In front of your mother and the Doctor, yes!

LAURA: In this case even my mother becomes a stranger—not to mention the Doctor. You seemed to be throwing him in my face!

GIORGIO: Because I cannot and will not believe that you refuse to accept his help now.

LAURA: Giorgio, look at me. Can't you look at me any more?

GIORGIO: If it's true that you don't want to do this thing, no! I want you to tell me at once, without fear of hurting me, what it is you want to do.

LAURA: What am I to do? It depends on you, Giorgio. On your decision.

GIORGIO: Do I need to tell you what my decision is? What can it be? Don't you understand it? Don't you feel it?

LAURA: I feel that you've suddenly turned against me. As if I . . . (*Quietly, with anguish.*) Oh, no!

GIORGIO: Then you refuse?

LAURA (*desperately, almost to herself*): Oh God! God! Was it all useless, then?

GIORGIO (*bewildered*): What was useless? What are you talking about? Answer me.

LAURA: So you can think of only one thing, and forget everything else?

GIORGIO: What do you expect me to think of at a time like this?

LAURA: Can't you see that for me it's just the opposite?

GIORGIO: The opposite? What?

LAURA (*as though absorbed, distant, savagely, slowly*): I have forgotten the one thing you remember. I have no recollection, no image of it: nothing. I saw nothing! I knew nothing. **Nothing**, you understand?

GIORGIO: Well?

LAURA (*with supplication*): Yet you don't . . . ? (*She waits for him to grasp her meaning. A long pause, then very quietly.*) What more is there for me to say if you have forgotten everything else?

GIORGIO: Ah, your love, you mean? So that's how it is, is it? You thought that if you surrounded me with your love—'enveloped' me with your caresses—I should believe!

LAURA (*with a cry*): No! (*Then, sickened with disappointment in him, she half groans.*) Oh!

GIORGIO: What then?

LAURA: You look for motives—but I didn't reason—I loved! I'm almost dead for love of you. I have made myself yours, as no other woman in the world has ever belonged to a man, and you know it. You can't possibly not have felt that I wanted to possess you completely, that I wanted myself to be all yours.

GIORGIO: Well, then?

LAURA (*crying out*): I didn't reason, I tell you!

GIORGIO: But what did you hope to do?

LAURA: Why, to . . . to wipe out . . .

GIORGIO: What? How?

LAURA (*after a moment, hopelessly*): Nothing. You are right.

It was madness.

GIORGIO: Yes, madness! You realise it now.

LAURA: Yes, but I am recovering from it—in fact, I'm already cured. But I warn you, you can no longer talk to me now as though I were a madwoman!

GIORGIO: That's just it, Laura—I want you to reason.

LAURA (*icily*): And if I do?

GIORGIO (*quietly—with compassion*): You'll see, I hope, that—unfortunately—it will be necessary for you to undergo ... we'll have to ask the Doctor to ... (*He does not complete the sentence.*)

LAURA: I see! Just to satisfy reason? And after you have cast in my teeth—with contempt and horror—all that I have given you of myself? All that you consider was merely cold calculation on my part: and ugly deception ...

GIORGIO: No, no, Laura—you ... you even called it madness yourself!

LAURA (*with a strange smile*): Ah, madness, yes! And I hoped that it had swept you up with me ... here among the plants that understand this madness of mine! Or that you would at least have asked me to agree to it, as a poor madwoman who doesn't realise what she is doing—the sacrifice of her life—; and who knows? Perhaps you would have got what you wanted. Because you cannot believe that I wanted to preserve in my body a being that I neither feel nor know as yet. I wanted to preserve love, to wipe out a brutal misfortune, not brutally, as you would like ...

GIORGIO: How then? How, in God's name?

LAURA: Can I tell you how if you don't see it for yourself?

GIORGIO: By accepting your madness?

LAURA (*with a cry from the depths of her soul*): Yes! All of me! So that you might see that I am all yours, in **your** son—the son made yours through my love for you! That—that is what I wanted!

GIORGIO (*drawing back—almost horrified*): Oh no!

LAURA: It's not possible: I see that now.

GIORGI: How can you expect me to accept such a suggestion?

LAURA: Then, instead, let me accept my misfortune.

GIORGIO: You?

LAURA: By myself, yes, my whole misfortune from beginning to end.

GIORGIO: Do you mean by that that you refuse?

LAURA: Why not—if after all I have given of myself I have not succeeded in blotting out that terrible day . . .

GIORGIO: Ah, no, Laura: you can't! You mustn't!

LAURA (*calmly*): Why can't I?

GIORGIO: After what you wanted to do?

LAURA: What did I want to do?

GIORGIO: You expected my love—after that!

LAURA (*scornfully*): For the sake of appearances—as you thought?

GIORGIO: But what about me, Laura? What will people think?

LAURA: Oh, don't worry. I shall have the courage that Zena had. It's a shame that—after the 'deception' I shan't be able to give my son to his real father!

GIORGIO: But you wanted to give him to me! Isn't that deception?

LAURA: You call it deception! I know that it was love.

GIORGIO: I tell you you can't!

LAURA: And how will you prevent me? By violence?

GIORGIO: If necessary—yes. (LAURA *goes to the centre door and calls.*)

LAURA: Mother! Mother! (*The door opens.* SIGNORA BETTI *and the* DOCTOR *enter hurriedly.*)

SIGNORA BETTI (*agitated*): Laura, my child?

ROMERI: What is it?

GIORGIO: Doctor, tell her that as she's my wife . . .

LAURA: I am no longer your wife! Mother, I am coming away with you.

GIORGIO: But it's not enough that you should go away!

LAURA (*proudly*): Why? What have I of yours?

GIORGIO (*only just audible. He is shattered*): Oh, my God! (*A pause.*)

LAURA: Come, Mother, we can go now.

GIORGIO (*a cry of exasperation and despair*): No! Laura! Laura! (*He utters her name the first time with anxious alarm, then imploring. He covers his face with hands and falls into a chair. A pause, then)*

LAURA (*her voice full of tenderness*): Giorgio . . . do you believe in me?

GIORGIO (*broken*): I can't! But I don't want to lose your love.

LAURA: But that is the very thing you must believe in!

GIORGIO: Believe? How? In what?

LAURA: Believe in what I have desired with all my being for your sake, what you too must desire! How can you not believe in it?

GIORGIO: Yes, yes . . . I believe in your love.

LAURA (*almost delirious*): What more do you want, then, if you believe in my love? There's nothing else in me but love. You are in me, and there's nothing else. Nothing else any more! Don't you feel it?

GIORGIO (*slowly*): Yes, yes . . .

LAURA (*radiantly happy*): Ah—then my love has won! It has won! My love!

THE CURTAIN FALLS

THE OTHER SON

L'Altro figlio

1923

Translated by
Bruce Penman

CHARACTERS

MARAGRAZIA
NINFAROSA
ROCCO TRUPÌA
A YOUNG DOCTOR
JACO SPINA
TINO LIGRECI

LA GIALLUZZA
LA Z'A MARASSUNTA
LA 'GNA TUZZA LA DIA
LA MARINESE
A GROUP OF CHILDREN

A group of gossiping
village women

"Z'a" is short for "Zia", meaning "Aunt"; " 'Gna" is short for
"Signora")

The scene is in Sicily, in the first decade of the twentieth century.

The last few cottages of the village of Fàrnia in Sicily, stand on the bend of a dismal little road which winds out among the neighbouring fields. The clay-walled, one-storey cottages stand a little apart from one another, each with a patch of garden behind it and a couple of steps leading up to the faded, rotting front door, which is left open to admit the light of day. To the left of the road, facing the others, is Ninfarosa's house, which is a little less ancient and decrepit.

As the curtain goes up, four village women are sitting in front of their cottage doors. LA GIALLUZZA is a little woman of about thirty, with hair that used to be blonde but is now a faded yellow, twisted up into a bun; LA Z'A MARASSUNTA is an old woman of about sixty, wearing a faded mourning dress of black cotton, with a black headscarf knotted under her chin; LA 'GNA TUZZA LA DIA is about forty, with permanently downcast eyes and a wailing voice; LA MARINESE is red-haired and flashy. All four of them are busy with darning, sorting vegetables, knitting and similar tasks; and they talk as they work. JACO SPINA, an old peasant, in shirt-sleeves, with a black knitted cap, is lying comfortably on his back a little way down the road, with his head resting on a donkey's pack-saddle, smoking his pipe and listening to the women. Some small boys, burnt almost black by the sun, are playing around.

LA GIALLUZZA: And there's another lot going this very evening!

LA 'GNA TUZZA (*in a wailing voice*): And good luck to them, poor boys!

LA MARINESE: They say more than twenty are going this time!

TINO LIGRECI *enters from between two cottages to the right; he is a young peasant who has recently finished his military service, with defiant manner, wide trousers and his cap on the side of his head.*

TINO (*addressing* Z'A MARASSUNTA): Good evening, Z'a Marassú. Can you tell me if the doctor's been through here? I know he was going out to see Rocco Trupía, at Pillar House.
Z'A MARASSUNTA: No, my son, he hasn't been this way. I haven't seen him, at least.
LA MARINESE: And nor have we. But why do you want him? Who is ill?
TINO: No one, thanks be to God. I wanted to ask him to look after my mother . . . (*Looking at the four women, he hesitates, and adds sadly.*) And I wanted to ask you too . . . to keep an eye on her from time to time. She's going to be all alone, poor woman.

Meanwhile MARAGRAZIA *has come out from behind Ninfarosa's house. She is over seventy years old; her face is covered with a dense network of wrinkles, and her everted eyelids are blood-red with constant weeping. A few wisps of hair, parted on top of her head, hang in small clusters over her ears. She looks like a heap of rags—greasy, unpleasant rags, tattered and torn and full of all the filth of the streets, rags from which all the colour has faded and which are never changed in summer or in winter. On her feet are a pair of hideous, leaky old boots, and her stockings are of coarse blue cotton.*

LA MARINESE (*to* TINO): So you are going . . . ?
TINO: Yes, I leave this evening with the rest of the party. But I'm not going to the same place. They are going to San Paolo; I'm going to Rosario di Santa Fé.*
MARAGRAZIA (*coming up behind him*): So you are on your way, too . . .

* *Translator's note:* In Argentina

TINO: Yes, I am! I'm going far, far away, where I'll never have to look at your face or listen to your weeping again, you stupid old faggot!

MARAGRAZIA (*looking fixedly at him*): And you're going to Rosario, you said? To Rosario di Santa Fé?

TINO: To Rosario—that's right. But why are you looking at me like that—as if you'd like to have the eyes out of my head?

MARAGRAZIA: No, no, my fine fellow, I don't want your eyes; though I do envy you them, because, when you reach Rosario, it's with them that you'll see . . . (*her chin trembles and she is shaken by a fit of silent sobbing*) my two boys, who are both there. Tell them the state I was in when you left. Tell them that if they don't come back at once, they won't find me here.

TINO (*sarcastically*): Yes, of course! As soon as we land! Everything happens very quickly over there. You just shout and the other fellow answers at once! But now let me go and look for the doctor.

MARAGRAZIA (*holding him back by one arm*): Wait a moment. If I give you you a letter for them, will you take it?

TINO (*impatiently*): Yes—you'd better give it to me now,

MARAGRAZIA: It's not ready yet. I'll get it written out at once by Ninfarosa, and take it round to your house. All right?

TINO: Very well, bring it round to me. (*Turning to* Z'A MARASSUNTA.) And now, in case we don't see each other again . . . (*his voice betrays his emotion*) give me your blessing, Z'a Marassú.

Z'A MARASSUNTA (*standing up and making the sign of the cross over his head*): God's blessing on you, my son! And may He be your guard and protector by land and by sea!

TINO (*turning to the other women and smiling to hide his emotion*): And I'll say good-bye to you too, then! (*He shakes hands with all three of them.*)

LA 'GNA TUZZA: I wish you a good journey, Tinù.

LA MARINESE: And good luck! And don't forget us!

LA GIALLUZZA: And come back soon and in good health and with a bag of money as big as this! (*Expansive gesture.*)

TINO: Thank you, thank you! Good health and prosperity to all those who remain here! (*Exit* TINO, *left.*)

Z'A MARASSUNTA: And he goes off and leaves his mother, the minute he gets back from the army!

LA' GNA TUZZA: And asks everyone else to look after her! (MARAGRAZIA *watches* TINO *out of sight, and then turns towards the other women.*)

MARAGRAZIA: Is Ninfarosa at home?

LA GIALLUZZA: Yes—knock, if you want her.

NINFAROSA (*calling from inside her house*): Who's that?

MARAGRAZIA: It's me—Maragrazia.

NINFAROSA (*as before*): I'm coming—wait a moment! (MARAGRAZIA *slowly lowers herself on to the step in front of* NINFAROSA's *door. She sits there and listens to the other women's talk, shaking her head and weeping.*)

LA GIALLUZZA: I hear that Saro Scoma is going too—leaving his wife here with three children.

LA 'GNA TUZZA (*in her usual wailing voice*): And a fourth one on the way!

LA MARINESE (*losing patience*): What a voice you've got there, neighbour! What a strain on the nerves! It really makes me feel quite queasy! Well, three and one make four; if they've done that bit of addition, it must be because they liked doing it and enjoyed it. And now they've got to pay the price. That's all.

JACO SPINA (*sitting up, with his big hands clasped in front of his chest*): If I were king (*spitting on the ground*)—if I were king, I wouldn't let a single letter—no, nor a message of any kind—come to Fàrnia from those foreign parts.

LA GIALLUZZA: Well said, Uncle Jaco Spina! And what would the poor wives and mothers do, with no news and no help coming in?

JACO SPINA: And a fine lot of help they get now! (*He spits again.*) The mothers go and work as servants and the wives go right off the rails! There are houses in the village where you can hear the cuckoo sing all the year round! Why don't they ever say anything in their letters about all the grief and trouble they find over there? It's only the good things they mention. Whenever a letter comes, all these ignorant young louts are like day-old chicks that hear a hen clucking in the distance—cluck! cluck! cluck! and they all troop off after her! And so there's no one left here to hoe or reap or prune— nothing but children, women and old men. I've got a bit of land, and I have to watch it suffering. What can I do (*holding out his arms*) with one pair of hands? And more and more of them troop off. I wish them rain in the face and a gale of wind! I hope they break their necks, the bastards!

NINFAROSA *comes out of her house. Black-haired and red- cheeked, she has dark, sparkling eyes and fiery, passionate lips; her body is strong and slim; her manner is cheerful and una- bashed. A red cotton scarf with a pattern of yellow half moons covers her shapely bosom; and she is wearing heavy, hoop- shaped gold ear-rings.*

NINFAROSA: Who's preaching the sermon today? Why, it's you, Uncle Jaco Spina! But really, Uncle Jaco, wouldn't it be best if we were left all alone in Fàrnia? Sanctity goes with solitude, they say! And we women will hoe the ground!

JACO SPINA: You women are only good for one thing.

NINFAROSA: And what's that, Uncle Jaco? Out with it!

JACO SPINA: Weeping . . . and one other thing.

NINFAROSA: So that makes two things we're good for! That's better! Not that I weep much, myself.

JACO SPINA: I know that, my girl! You didn't weep for long when your first husband died.

NINFAROSA: That's true—but if I'd died first, Uncle Jaco, wouldn't he have married again? Well, then! Besides, there's someone here (*indicating* MARAGRAZIA) who does the weeping for all of us.

JACO SPINA: That's because the old woman has too much water to get rid of; and so she gets rid of some of it through her eyes. (*He rises to his feet, picks up the saddle and goes off through a gap between two cottages.*)

MARAGRAZIA: Do you expect me not to weep, when I've lost two sons, the finest lads you'll ever see?

NINFAROSA: Fine lads they must be, and well worth weeping for! They're rolling in money over there, while you starve in the street like a beggar!

MARAGRAZIA (*shrugging her shoulders*): There's children for you! They've no idea what their mother suffers.

NINFAROSA: But I can't see the point of all this moaning and groaning, when you made life such hell for them. From what I hear, you drove them away from home. (*Deeply shocked*, MARAGRAZIA *rises to her feet and strikes her breast with her fist.*)

MARAGRAZIA: I drove them away? Who could have said a thing like that?

NINFAROSA: Whoever it was, they did say it!

MARAGRAZIA: It's a dirty lie! Drive away my sons, indeed! When I think what I've done for them . . .

Z'A MARASSUNTA (*to* MARAGRAZIA): Don't take any notice of her!

LA MARINESE: Can't you see that she's joking?

NINFAROSA: Yes, I'm joking, I'm joking! Don't get excited—and tell me what you wanted, when you knocked at my door just now.

MARAGRAZIA: Why, yes—I wondered if you'd do me the favour you've done me before . . .

NINFAROSA: . . . and write a letter for you! Is that it?

MARAGRAZIA: If you'll do it for me! I'll take it to Tino Ligreci, who's leaving for Rosario di Santa Fé this evening.

NINFAROSA: So Tino's going too, is he? Well, good luck to him! Let's get this letter done quickly, though; I'm doing some sewing, and I'm nearly out of thread for the machine. I must go and buy some more.

MARAGRAZIA: Yes—I'll tell you what to say . . . Tell them about the cottage, the same as last time.

NINFAROSA: Four shaky walls of clay and reeds?

MARAGRAZIA: Yes—I was thinking about it again last night. Write like this: 'My dear sons, you remember the old cottage, that's stood so long and is still standing? Well, your mother will make a free gift of it to you in her lifetime, if you come home to her now.'

NINFAROSA: That should fetch them, all right! Especially if it's true that they've made their fortunes! I'm only afraid they'll arrive in such a rush that they'll knock the old cottage down before they can take possession of it . . . See what I mean?

MARAGRAZIA: Why, my child, a heap of stones in your own land is worth more than a palace in foreign parts. (*She takes a sheet of cheap writing-paper and an envelope out of the bosom of her dress.*) Here, take this, and write it all down.

NINFAROSA: Yes, give me the paper. You can sit there on the doorstep while you're waiting—if you come in, you'll make everything dirty. (NINFAROSA *takes the paper and goes indoors.*)

MARAGRAZIA (*sitting down again on the step*): You're right! You're right! You have a fine clean house; I wander about in the fields. One of these days you people will look for me and you'll find me eaten by the rats in that little cottage of mine.

NINFAROSA (*calling out from indoors*): I've written to them about the cottage. Is there anything else you'd like me to say?

MARAGRAZIA: Yes, please. Write this: 'Dear sons! Now that winter is approaching, your poor old mother is trembling with the cold. Be good boys and send her something—not much, ten lire perhaps— so that she can buy herself . . . '(*Enter NIN-FAROSA, hurriedly. She has put on her shawl, ready to go to the shop, and is tucking the folded sheet of paper into its envelope.*)

NINFAROSA (*thrusting letter into* MARAGRAZIA's *hand*): Here you are! Finished! All done! Take it!

MARAGRAZIA (*painfully astonished by all this sudden haste*): Finished, did you say? But how . . . ?

NINFAROSA: Yes, all finished, including the message about the ten lire! You can be sure of that! And now I must go. (*Exit NINFAROSA, between the first and second cottages.*)

MARAGRAZIA (*as before*): But how could she she write it all down so quickly, before I'd even said what I wanted to buy with the ten lire?

LA MARINESE: She knew it was a dress you wanted, because she's written the same message for you at least twenty times! (*Perplexed and unconvinced,* MARAGRAZIA *stands there*

with the envelope in her hands. Enter the young DOCTOR
along the narrow road from the fields.)

DOCTOR (*addressing* LA GIALLUZZA): Excuse me—I'm
looking for a certain Rocco Trupía, at Pillar House. Could
you tell me where it is, please?

LA GIALLUZZA: Why, Doctor, didn't you see it as you came
along the road? It's up there at the very end of the village.
There's no mistaking it, because there's a bit of an ancient
pillar at the corner of the wall.

DOCTOR: I didn't see any ancient pillar.

Z'A MARASSUNTA: The fact is, Doctor, that there's a sort of
hedge of prickly pear between the wall and the road, so that
if you didn't know the pillar was there you wouldn't see it.

DOCTOR: Well, I don't fancy wading through all that dust a
second time. I'm not going back there now. I'd be grateful if
you'd send one of these boys to tell Rocco Trupía that the
Doctor wants to speak to him.

Z'A MARASSUNTA: Is it about his aunt? The poor woman! Is
she worse?

DOCTOR: She's no worse, and no better. What he's got to do
is to make her go into hospital in the city—force her to go,
if necessary. She can't have the treatment she needs at home.
I've already written out the application to the Mayor's office
to get her admitted to hospital.

LA GIALLUZZA (*calling to one of the boys playing in the
road*): Calicchio! Here's a job for you! You know Pillar
House? Run there as fast as you can and ask for Uncle Rocco
Trupía. Tell him he's wanted here. Say the Doctor wants to
speak to him. (*The boy nods and runs off along the road
leading to the fields.*)

DOCTOR: Thanks very much. When he arrives, please send him
along to my house. I'm going there now. (*As he turns to go out
past* NINFAROSA's *house*, MARAGRAZIA *speaks to him.*)

MARAGRAZIA: Excuse me, Doctor. Would you be so kind as
to read this letter out to me?

Z'A MARASSUNTA (*quickly, much concerned to prevent the*
DOCTOR *seeing the letter*): No, no, Maragrazia! Don't
bother the Doctor—he's in a hurry!

LA MARINESE (*similarly concerned*): Don't listen to her, Doctor!

DOCTOR: I'm not in a hurry. Why shouldn't I listen? (*Turning to* MARAGRAZIA.) Give me the letter! (*He takes the envelope, extracts the sheet of paper, and prepares to read it. Then he stares at the old woman as if she were playing a joke on him. The four other women begin to laugh.*)

DOCTOR (*to* MARAGRAZIA): What **is** all this?

MARAGRAZIA: Is it very difficult to read . . . ?

DOCTOR: How can I read something that isn't there? There's nothing written on this piece of paper.

MARAGRAZIA (*amazed and indignant*): Nothing? How can there be nothing?

DOCTOR: Nothing but half-a-dozen meaningless squiggles, zig-zag lines drawn at random with the pen. Here, you can see for yourself.

MARAGRAZIA: Ah, I might have known! She hasn't written anything at all! The wicked hussy! Why did she play this cruel trick on me?

DOCTOR (*indignantly addressing the four laughing women*): Who did this? And what are you laughing at?

Z'A MARASSUNTA: She's found out! At last!

LA 'GNA TUZZA: It took her long enough!

LA MARINESE: Ninfarosa, the dressmaker, plays this trick on her every time!

LA GIALLUZZA: Just to get rid of her! To get her to go away!

MARAGRAZIA: Ah, Doctor, so this is why my sons have never answered my letters! She's never written anything down properly in all the letters she's done for me. So that's why it is! They don't know about the bad way I'm in. They don't know I'm dying on my feet for longing to see them again. And to think that I've been blaming them, while all the time it was this wicked hussy here that was playing a trick on me! (*She begins to weep.*)

Z'A MARASSUNTA: But it wasn't out of wickedness that she did it at all, Doctor!

DOCTOR (*to* MARAGRAZIA): Come on now! Don't give up hope! Come to my house a little later on, and I'll write the

letter myself for you to send to your sons! But you'd better
go now! (*He takes her by the arm and affectionately urges
her to go.*)

MARAGRAZIA (*going off left, behind* NINFAROSA's *house,
still weeping*): Dear God! How could anyone play a dirty
trick like that on a poor mother? What a thing to do! What a
terrible thing! (*Exit* MARAGRAZIA. *Re-enter* NINFAROSA
*between the first and second cottages, in time to see the old
woman leave the stage, while the other four women, with a
touch of embarrassed regret, follow her with their gaze.*)

NINFAROSA: Has she found out, by any chance?

DOCTOR: So it's you, is it?

NINFAROSA: Good morning, Doctor!

DOCTOR: Good morning be damned! Aren't you ashamed of
yourself for playing this cruel game with a poor mother?

NINFAROSA: Before you condemn me, you should hear what
I've got to say.

DOCTOR: What can you say?

NINFAROSA: She's mad, Doctor, she's mad! Don't take it to
heart so much!

DOCTOR: And what pleasure can there be in deceiving a lunatic?

NINFAROSA: No pleasure at all; it's more like telling fibs to
children to keep them happy. The madness got into her brain
after her two sons went off to South America. She won't
admit that they've forgotten about her, which is the truth. For
years past she's been sending them one letter after another.
I've been pretending to write them for her. I just put a couple
of squiggles on a piece of paper; the boys who go off to South
America promise to take them and deliver them for her; and
the poor old creature takes it all for gospel. Ah, Doctor, if we
all looked at it the way you do, what would happen? We'd
all be drowned in the great flood of her tears. I have my
troubles too, you know. My gay spark of a husband is over
there, and do you know what he had the nerve to do? He sent
me a picture of himself and his girl-friend with their heads
close together like this, and their hands tightly clasped—give
me your hand for a moment, Doctor—like that. And they're

laughing their heads off at the world in general, and at me
most of all, since they sent me the picture. But I look at my
own hands—see how white they are, real dressmaker's hands,
with a dimple for each finger—and I take the world as it
comes!

LA GIALLUZZA: You're a lucky woman, Ninfaró!

NINFAROSA: Lucky? Because I take the world as it comes?
Why, that's a virtue you could just as easily have yourself!
And once you've got it, everything goes well for you!

Z'A MARASSUNTA: Eh, but you're quick off the mark, all
right!

NINFAROSA: Perhaps you people are a bit slow! But you can
say anything you like about me—it's like water off a duck's
back.

DOCTOR: You all know where your next meal is coming from,
at least. But that poor old woman . . .

NINFAROSA: Maragrazia, d'you mean? She could be as well
off as anybody! She could be waited on hand and foot, if she
wanted to. But she doesn't! Anyone here will tell you the
same. (*Chorus of* 'Yes! Yes! It's true!' *from the other women.*)

NINFAROSA: If only she'd go and live with her son!

DOCTOR: What was that? . . . Has she got another son, then?

LA MARINESE: Yes, Doctor. Her other son is Rocco Trupía,
the man you wanted to see.

DOCTOR: Is he? Then the old woman must be the sister of the
other lunatic who won't let me send her to hospital?

LA GIALLUZZA: No, Doctor, she's her sister-in-law.

NINFAROSA: But heaven help anyone who says so to Maragrazia! She won't hear her son's name mentioned, or any of
his relations on the father's side.

DOCTOR: It sounds as if he must have treated her pretty badly!

NINFAROSA: I don't think so. But here he comes; you can ask
him yourself.

Enter ROCCO TRUPÍA *along the road from the fields, with the
boy who went to fetch him. He has the heavy walk of a peasant,
stooping and bow-legged, with one hand in the small of his
back. He is red-haired, fair-skinned and very freckled. From*

*time to time there is a sullen gleam in his sunken eyes. He comes
up to the* DOCTOR. *His hand goes up to his black knitted cap
and pushes it back by way of salute.*

ROCCO: I kiss your honour's hand and await your honour's
   orders.
DOCTOR: I wanted to speak to you about your aunt.
ROCCO: About sending her to hospital? Don't think of such a
   thing, your honour! Let her die in peace in her own bed!
DOCTOR: You're like all the others! You think it's a dishonour
   to take your aunt to a hospital where they'll make her well again!
ROCCO (*clasping his hands together and waving them to and
   fro*): Make her well again, sir? Poor people don't get well in
   hospital! And she'd die in desperation, without the comfort
   of having her own things around her! She won't go to hospital, and I won't take her there—not if you offered me a
   hundred pounds. She's been a mother to me!
DOCTOR: Yes, and about your mother . . .
ROCCO (*grimly cutting him short*): Has your honour any other
   instructions for me? I'm ready to do what you say. But if your
   honour wants to talk about my mother, I must bid you good
   day and get back to my work. (*He turns away; but the* DOC-
   TOR *holds him back.*)
DOCTOR: Wait a moment! I know it isn't your fault . . .
ROCCO (*abruptly*): Will you come to my house, sir? It's not
   far—just up the road. It's only a poor peasant's house; but,
   as you're a doctor, you must be used to that. I'd like to show
   you the bed I keep always made up and ready for that . . .
   worthy old woman. (I can't call her less than that, since she
   is my mother!) And you can ask these good neighbours of
   mine if it isn't true that I've always told my wife and my
   children to respect and honour her as if she were the Madonna
   herself (*making the sign of the cross and dropping his voice*)
   whose name I am not worthy to pronounce. I'd like to know
   what I've ever done to my mother, to make her shame me like
   this in front of the whole village. I was brought up by my
   father's family from the very day I was born, because she
   wouldn't even give me the first milk from her breasts for her

own comfort. Yet I've always respected her as my mother. And when I say the word 'mother', this (*suddenly taking off his cap and falling to his knees*) is what I mean by it, Doctor! For me, 'mother' is a holy word. (*He rises to his feet.*) As soon as those wretched sons of hers went off to South America, I went to fetch her, to take her into my own household, where I and the rest of my family would have done whatever she wanted. But it was no good. She preferred to beg her bread in the village street, making a spectacle of herself to everyone else and bringing shame on me! I swear this to you, Doctor: if either of those wretched louts ever comes back to Fàrnia, I'll kill him! I'll be revenged for the shame they've brought on me and the bitterness that's poisoned my life for fourteen years! I'll kill them, as sure as I stand here talking to you before these good women and these innocent children! (*His features distorted by passion, his eyes bloodshot,* ROCCO *wipes the foam from his lips with his forearm.*)

DOCTOR: Ah, but now I can see why your mother refuses to come and live with you. It's because of this hatred you have for your brothers!

ROCCO: Hatred, d'you say? It's true that I hate them now; but before they went away I respected them as elder brothers and cared for them more than for my own children. And they treated me like Cain treated Abel. They never did any work, so I had to work for three. They would come and tell me they had nothing in the house for supper, that our mother would be going to bed hungry—and I gave them money. They got drunk, they threw the money away on loose women—and I gave them more. When they went off to South America, I worked my fingers to the bone for them. Anyone in the village will tell you the same.

THE NEIGHBOURS: Yes, he's telling you the truth, poor lad . . . He went hungry himself to feed them.

DOCTOR: But in that case, why . . . ?

ROCCO (*with a grimace*): Why, do you ask? Because my mother says I'm not her son!

DOCTOR (*astonished*): Not her son? But how . . .

ROCCO: Doctor, you'd best get the women here to explain it to you. I've no time. The men are waiting for me up there with the mules laden with dung for the fields. I must get on with my work; and, as you can see, I'm all upset. Once again, I kiss your honour's hand. (*Exit* ROCCO, *stooping, bow-legged, with one hand in the small of his back, along the road to the fields.*)

NINFAROSA: What he says is the truth, poor fellow! And though he's ugly and always has that surly expression, with an evil-looking glint in his eyes, there's no wickedness in him at all!

LA 'GNA TUZZA: And what a worker he is!

LA MARINESE: That's right! His work, his wife and his children are all he lives for! And he never says a word to anyone.

LA GIALLUZZA: He's got a fine small-holding on lease up at Pillar House, which brings him in a bit.

Z'A MARASSUNTA: That crazy old woman could live like a queen, if she wanted to!—and here she is again, still weeping! (*Re-enter* MARAGRAZIA *from behind* NINFAROSA's *house, with another sheet of writing-paper in her hand.*)

MARAGRAZIA (*to the DOCTOR*): I've bought the paper for the letter, if your honour will be kind enough to write it for me . . .

DOCTOR: Yes, I'll write it for you. But I've just had a word with your son. Now tell me: why did you conceal the fact that you had another son here in the village, when I spoke to you before?

MARAGRAZIA (*terrified*): No, no, for heaven's sake, don't talk to me about him, Doctor! Don't talk about him! I come out in a cold sweat when you mention my other son! Don't talk to me about him!

DOCTOR: But why? What wrong has he done you? Tell me!

MARAGRAZIA: He's done nothing, Doctor, nothing at all! To be fair to him, he's never done me any wrong.

NINFAROSA (*bringing out a chair and offering it to the DOC-TOR*): Sit down, sir; you must be tired after all the time you've been on your feet.

DOCTOR (*sitting down*): Yes, thank you; I am a bit weary. (*Turning to* MARAGRAZIA.) Well? If he hasn't done you any harm . . .

MARAGRAZIA: See how I'm shaking all over? I can't talk about it. You see, Doctor, he's no son of mine!

DOCTOR: No son of yours? What do you mean? Are you really mad, or just plain stupid? Didn't you give birth to him?

MARAGRAZIA: Yes, sir, I did. And perhaps I am stupid. I'm not mad, though. I wish to heaven I were; then I shouldn't suffer so much . . . There are some things your honour can't know about, because you're too young. I'm a white-haired old woman, with a lifetime of suffering behind me; and the things I've seen! I've seen things that you couldn't even begin to imagine!

DOCTOR: What have you seen? Tell me about it!

MARAGRAZIA: You may have read it in a book—how there was a time, many years ago, when every city and every hamlet rebelled against all the laws of God and man!

DOCTOR: You mean, the time of the Revolution?*

MARAGRAZIA: That's it, your honour. They opened the doors of every prison in the country! It was as if the wrath of God were raging through the whole land. Out came the worst robbers, out came the blackest murderers—wild beasts thirsting for blood, animals maddened by years of captivity. There was one special one, called Cola Camizzi, who was the worst of them all. He was a brigand and a leader of brigands. He killed God's creatures for fun, like a boy killing flies. He said he did it to test the powder, or to see if his gun was in good working order. He came raging through the district till he came to Fàrnia. He'd already got quite a sizeable gang of peasants with him; but that wasn't enough. He wanted more recruits; and he killed all the men who refused to go with him. I'd been married just two or three years; I'd already had my two elder sons, who are in South America now—my own dear boys! We lived at Pozzetto, where my husband, God rest his

---

* *Translator's note:* The Revolution of 1860, led by Garibaldi.

soul, worked as a sharecropper. Cola Camizzi came to Pozzetto, too, and dragged my husband away by brute force. Two
days later he came back to me, more dead than alive; it was
as if he were another person. He couldn't speak, and his eyes
seemed to be full of the terrible things that he'd seen. He kept
trying to hide his hands, poor lad, out of horror at what those
brutes had made him do. I felt my heart turn over inside me
when I saw him standing in front of me looking like that!
'Mino, dear, what have you done?' I screamed at the poor
fellow: but he couldn't get out a word. 'So you ran away from
them?' I said. 'And if they catch you again now, what will
happen? They'll kill you!' I knew in my heart that it was true.
But he said nothing—he just sat by the fire, with his hands
hidden under his jacket, like this (*folding her arms.*) He
looked at me with unseeing eyes; and in the end all he said
was 'I'd be better dead!.' Those were the only words I heard
from him. He stayed hidden indoors for three days. On the
fourth day he went out; we were poor people and he had to
work. He went out into the fields. When evening came, he
didn't come home. I waited and waited. Oh God, I knew what
had happened—I'd been expecting it! But I thought to myself: 'Perhaps they haven't killed him; perhaps they've just
taken him back into their gang!.' Six days later news came
that Cola Camizzi and his gang were at Montelusa, in a
monastery that belonged to the Redemptorist Fathers, who
had left the place not long before. I ran like a mad thing all
the way from Pozzetto to Montelusa, which is over six miles.
There was a wind blowing that day the like of which I've
never seen since. It sounds foolish to talk about seeing the
wind; but this was a wind you really could see! And it
sounded as if the souls of all the people who had been mur-
dered were screaming together to God and man for vengeance. I screamed louder than the wind, as it blustered about
me and tore at my clothes; but I let it carry me along—and I
flew. It took me barely an hour to reach the monastery, high
up among the black poplars. Alongside the monastery build-
ings was a big walled courtyard. The way into it was through
a tiny door, which was half hidden—I can see it now!—by

the trailing branches of a caper bush rooted in the wall above.
I picked up a stone to knock with. I knocked and knocked,
but they didn't want to let me in. But I kept on, and in the
end they opened the door. And then I saw . . . Oh God, what
did I see? . . . In their hands . . . those murderers . . . (*Choking
with horror,* MARAGRAZIA *is unable to continue; but she
raises one hand and makes the motions of throwing something.*)

DOCTOR (*who has gone very pale*): Go on!

MARAGRAZIA: They were playing . . . in that courtyard . . .
playing bowls . . . with men's heads . . . all black and muddy
. . . they picked them up and held them by the hair . . . One of
them was my husband's head . . . Cola Camizzi had it in his
hand, and he held it up and showed it to me. (*She utters a
terrible cry and hides her face in her hands.*) The horror of
it was too much even for those murderous brutes. When Cola
Camizzi seized me by the throat to stop me screaming, one
of them sprang at him in a fury; and then four, five, ten of
them took courage from the first one, and went for him too.
They worried him like a pack of dogs. They'd had enough of
it; they'd had more than they could stand of his ferocious
tyranny. I had the satisfaction of seeing his throat cut by his
own companions, before my very eyes!

THE NEIGHBOURS (*all together*): His throat cut, and serve
him right!—Murderer!—Gallows-bird!—God is not mocked!

DOCTOR (*after a pause*): But your son . . . ?

MARAGRAZIA: Wait a moment, sir. The man who was the
first to rebel, the man who defended me, was called Marco
Trupía.

DOCTOR: Ah! So Rocco Trupía . . .

MARAGRAZIA: . . . is his son. But just think, your honour—
how could I be that man's wife, after all I'd seen? He took
me by force; he kept me tied up for three months, and gagged
too, to stop me screaming. When he came near me, I bit him.
At the end of three months the police came looking for him.
They put him back in prison, and he died there not long after.
But he left me the mother of his child. I swear to you, Doctor,
I was ready to tear out my own guts rather than to bear his

child! I knew that I couldn't even hold it in my arms. The thought of giving it the breast made me scream like a mad-woman. I nearly died. My mother, God rest her soul, didn't even let me see the baby; he was taken away to his father's family, who brought him up ... Now aren't I right, Doctor, to say that he's no son of mine?

DOCTOR: Maybe. But how is he to blame?

MARAGRAZIA: He isn't to blame at all, Doctor! And no word against him has ever passed my lips! Never, never! In fact, he's ... But what can I do, when the very sight of him, even in the distance, makes me shake like a leaf? He's just like his father—even the voice is the same. It isn't my fault—it's the blood in my veins that rebels!—And now, your honour (*timidly holding out the sheet of writing-paper*), you did very kindly say you'd help me with this ...

DOCTOR (*standing up*): Yes, of course. Come along to my house with me.

Z'A MARASSUNTA: Poor Maragrazia! I hope it does some good!

MARAGRAZIA (*suddenly aggressive*): It will! It will! It's only because of her (*pointing to* NINFAROSA) that my boys aren't here with me now!

DOCTOR: Come on, then! Let's go!

MARAGRAZIA (*quickly*): I'm coming! A nice, long letter ... (*She follows the DOCTOR off stage, with her hands clasped as if in prayer.*)

MARAGRAZIA: 'My dear sons: your poor little mother ... '

CURTAIN

BIBLIOGRAPHY

The following is a list of Pirandello's plays with the date of the first Italian performance. The English title is given where the play has been translated:

1910 *La morsa* (The Vise)
    Lumìe di Sicilia (Limes from Sicily)
1913 *Il dovere del medico* (The Doctor's Duty)
1915 *Se non così*
1916 *Pensaci, Giacomino!* (Think it Over, Giacomino!)
    Liolà (Liolà)
1917 *Così è se vi pare* (Right You Are, If You Think You Are)
    Il berretto a sonagli
    La giara (The Jar)
    Il pacere dell 'onesta' (The Pleasure of Honesty)
    L'Innesto (The Grafting)
1918 *Ma non è una cosa seria*
    Il giuoco delle parti (The Rules of the Game)
1919 *La patente*
    L'uomo, la bestia, e la virtu'
1920 *Tutto per bene* (All for the Best)
    Come prima, meglio di prima
    Cece' (Chee-Chee)
    La Signora Morli, una e due
1921 *Sei personaggi in cerca d'autore* (Six Characters in Search of an Author)
1922 *Enrico IV* (Henry IV)
    All'uscita (At the Gate)
    L'Imbecille (The Imbecile)
    Vestire gli ignudi (Clothe the Naked)
1923 *L'Uomo dal fiore in bocca* (The Man with the Flower in his Mouth)
    La vita che ti diedi (The Life I Gave Thee)
    L'Altra figlio (The Other Son)
1924 *Ciascuno a suo modo* (Each in His Own Way)
1925 *Sagra del signore della nave* (Our Lord of the Ship)
1927 *Diana e la tuda*
    L'Amico delle mogli
    Bellavita (Bellavita)
1928 *Scamandro*
    La nuova colonia
1929 *O di uno ò di nessuno*
    Lazzaro (Lazarus)
1930 *Come tu mi vuoi* (As You Desire Me)
    Questa sera si recita a soggetto (Tonight We Improvise)
1932 *Trovarsi*
1933 *Quando si e' equalcuno*
1934 *La favola del figlio cambiato*

1935 *Non si sa come*
1936 *Sogno (ma forse no)* (Dream, But Perhaps Not)
1937 *I giganti della montagna* (The Mountain Giants)